Davenport's Georgia Wills and Estate Planning Legal Forms

DAVENPORT'S GEORGIA WILLS AND ESTATE PLANNING LEGAL FORMS

2024 EDITION

written by attorneys Alex Russell and Beth Farmer

**SEE BOOKS AND LEGAL FORMS AT
WWW.DAVENPORTPUBLISHING.COM**

COPYRIGHT © 2024 -- ALEX RUSSELL

CREATIVE COMMONS LICENSE. This work is also licensed under a Creative Commons Attribution-NonCommercial-NoDerivatives 4.0 International License.

GOVERNMENT WORKS. No claim is made to copyright or ownership of government materials.

SOME STANDARD FORMS. No copyright or ownership is claimed of "standard" forms or leading forms for the state which are provided in this book, but fair use and privilege to use is claimed. Makers of such forms (often a state agency or hospital) have agreed by word, act, and implication the forms may be used and copied if no profit is sought and no substantial changes made to them. Such makers if not a lawyer or law firm are barred from profit or advantage in practicing law by making forms then limiting use. Forms and other related materials are used here for educational purposes only. Authors strongly believe in a religious duty to help people and do charity.

PUBLICATION DATA
(informal, library may use different data)

Names: Russell, Alex, 1972- author; Farmer, Beth, 1975- author

Title: Davenport's Georgia Wills And Estate Planning Legal Forms 2024 Edition

Other Titles: Davenport's Wills

Description: Davenport Publishing 2024

Suggested Identifiers: 9798370044083, LCCN 2021909030, 9798748423373

Subjects: LCSH: Wills--United States;
Wills--United States--Forms;
Estate Planning--United States;
Legal Forms

Classification: LFF KF755 .C55 2024 (or as library chooses)
DDC 346.73 Rus--dc24 (or as library chooses)

9 8 7 6 5 4 3 2 1 0 0 0 0 0 2 4

PERMISSION TO COPY AND USE BOOKS FOR FREE

To help people and groups publisher and authors of the book allow mostly free use by giving all a "Creative Commons Attribution-NonCommercial-NoDerivatives 4.0 International License".

Basically, as the image below says, any copying or use is OK if it still shows it is <u>by</u> the authors, is <u>non-commercial</u> (nc) with no price charged, and has <u>no derivatives (nd)</u> so no big changes.

Most users face no limit on copying, using, holding in library to loan out, or giving out copies.

Permission is given to change margins and formatting, do small changes, and cut any blank pages that may occur (but double-check page numbers and table of contents page numbers).

Printing on only 1 side of pages avoids complication of writing on back. Text margins are .75 inches. To do a book not a pamphlet increase left (inside) and decrease right (outside) margins.

Users can design a cover they like but the book title and author names must still appear on it.

Email questions to **davenportpress@gmail.com** .

(This work licensed under a Creative Commons Attribution-NonCommercial-NoDerivatives 4.0 International License.)

FOR FREE COPIES USE WWW.DAVENPORTPUBLISHING.COM OR BUY AT AMAZON.COM.

WARNING

THIS PUBLICATION IS NOT A SUBSTITUTE FOR LEGAL ADVICE. Publisher and authors say and warn this publication is not giving any legal, accounting, or other professional services or advice, which if wanted can be obtained by consulting in person an attorney or some other professional. **No attorney-client relationship or any relationship creating a duty or obligation is agreed to or created by the purchase or use of this publication or forms.**

BOOKS AND FORMS FOR OTHER STATES ARE AVAILABLE.
SEE WWW.DAVENPORTPUBLISHING.COM FOR INFORMATION.

CHAPTER	TABLE OF CONTENTS	PAGE NUMBER
CHAPTER 1 - LIST OF FORMS, BOOK BASICS, AND INFORMATION FORM		1
CHAPTER 2 - LEGAL TERMS AND PROPERTY LAW BASICS		6
CHAPTER 3 - WILL BASICS		8
CHAPTER 4 - WILL GIFTS INCLUDING RESIDUE CLAUSE		10
CHAPTER 5 - DEBT, MARRIAGE, AND YOUNG CHILD ISSUES		15
CHAPTER 6 - BASIC IDEAS ABOUT HEALTH CARE FORMS		18

WILL RELATED FORMS

CHAPTER 7 - FORM 1: WILL (STANDARD)		19
CHAPTER 8 - FORM 2: WILL (GUARDIAN)		23
CHAPTER 9 - FORM 3: SELF-PROVING AFFIDAVIT		27
CHAPTER 10 - FORM 4: TANGIBLE PERSONAL PROPERTY GIFT LIST		29

HEALTH CARE FORMS

CHAPTER 11 - FORM 5: ADVANCE DIRECTIVE FOR HEALTH CARE		31
CHAPTER 12 - FORM 6: DO NOT RESUSCITATE		40

GIVING POWER FORMS

CHAPTER 13 - FORM 7: STATUTORY FORM POWER OF ATTORNEY		46
CHAPTER 14 - FORM 8: POWER OF ATTORNEY TO DELEGATE THE POWER AND AUTHORITY FOR THE CARE OF A CHILD		53
CHAPTER 15 - FORM 9: DESIGNATION TO CONTROL REMAINS		59
APPENDIX: HOW TO GET FORMS AND SAMPLE FILLED OUT FORMS		61

CHAPTER 1
LIST OF FORMS, BOOK BASICS, AND INFORMATION FORM

ESTATE PLANNING CONTROLS THINGS IF LATER ABSENT, SICK, OR DEAD

By Davenport Publishing this book covers Estate Planning in Georgia. This is doing legal documents now to control health care, property, money, children, and funeral if a person is later absent, sick, or dead.

ESTATE PLANNING MOSTLY IS DOING SIMPLE THINGS IN 3 AREAS

Estate Planning is mostly doing things in 3 areas: <u>Will Related</u>, <u>Health Care</u>, and <u>Giving Power</u>. In this book and at www.davenportpublishing.com are legal forms for Georgia. <u>Most people use just a few forms</u>.

WILL RELATED FORMS

<u>**Form 1. Will (Standard)**</u> – a Will (also called a "Last Will And Testament") lets a person control things after their death like who gets money and property, who is Executor, and if easier legal options can be used.

<u>**Form 2. Will (Guardian)**</u> – this is Will a with part added to name a person as "Guardian" to if needed care for any minor child under 18 and also manage their property and money till age 18.

<u>**Form 3. Self-Proving Affidavit**</u> – this helps later show a Will was witnessed right so legally can be used.

<u>**Form 4. Tangible Personal Property Gift List**</u> – lets a person easily after a Will is done write more gifts to occur after death of "tangible personal property" like furniture, clothing, appliances, vehicles, and jewelry.

HEALTH CARE FORMS

<u>**Form 5. Advance Directive For Health Care**</u> – lets a person name someone "Health Care Agent" in case needed to later control health care, and also write health care instructions (including about stopping care <u>if later</u> doctors say a person is so ill more treatment won't help -- many people call this a "Living Will").

<u>**Form 6. Do Not Resuscitate**</u> – this is actually 2 forms that <u>immediately</u> block most health care and they are very short so paramedics and other people can read and follow them quickly either in or out of a facility.

GIVING POWER FORMS

<u>**Form 7. Statutory Form Power Of Attorney**</u> – lets power over money, property, and more be shared during life with someone (who often is a spouse, adult child, or good friend) so they have power to do things.

<u>**Form 8. Power Of Attorney To Delegate The Power And Authority For The Care Of A Child**</u> – lets a parent share power over a child under 18 with a person so they can control a child's health care and more.

<u>**Form 9. Designation To Control Remains**</u> – can name a person to control funeral and related issues and lets instructions be given (often this form is only done if person doesn't want close family to run things).

PERSON HAS POWER TO CONTROL THESE THINGS BUT IT'S OFTEN NOT VITAL

Estate Planning to control health care, property, money, children, funeral, and similar things if a person is absent, sick, or dead is usually easy to do because a person mostly has full power to control these things. Given this usually judges, doctors, and other people mostly just ask: **"Based on what a person wrote what did they likely want done?"** It is also easy to do because simple legal documents can do most things and simple words can also be used (like listing some property and putting a few names). And despite what many people say often Estate Planning is not worth a lot of effort or money since it many not greatly change the costs, taxes, delays, and later work that's needed. For young adults or parents the benefits of costly Estate Planning seem low since only about 4% of people die before age 50, and only 0.2% of children under 19 had 2 parents die to probably need a Guardian. See Social Security Census Tables by Felicitie Bell. Many people to help family more spend more energy and money on getting $100,000 or so of life insurance.

GEORGIA LAW ON ESTATE PLANNING COVERS MOST PEOPLE HERE

This book is only for Georgia since Estate Planning laws and legal documents do vary among the states. Georgia law applies to Estate Planning usually if a person: a) has a main residence here (their "domicile"), or b) resided here and left but always keeps firm plans to leave any new place (even if a person rents a home elsewhere like some students, military, and workers). Many people also make sure to do health care forms for the state a health facility they use is located in. Most immigrants of any kind can do Estate Planning here.

BOOK IS SHORT, QUICKLY SHOWS LEGAL FORMS, AND USES EMPHASIS

This short book may read rough but it can be read fast and it also quickly shows people many legal forms. For emphasis some paragraph titles, boxes, and underlining is used, some small words are skipped, and end quote marks is put before punctuation. Though optional some legal words like Will and Testator are capitalized.

THIS BOOK COVERS THE MAIN LEGAL IDEAS AND SHOULD SUIT MOST PEOPLE

This book covers the main U.S. legal ideas on Estate Planning and the main ways Georgia law is different. This book can't cover all legal issues but should suit most people without some strange situations or wishes. Strange situations or wishes that may need research or a lawyer include: a) strange gift wishes for property and money, b) wealth over $5 million, c) big medical concerns like extreme age, d) property or money going to a person with a disability or special needs, and e) wish to move or hide assets to qualify for government help.

FORMS MAKE BINDING LEGAL DOCUMENTS AND BOOK HAS STANDARD FORMS

Legal forms are good at most things involved in Estate Planning and can make binding legal documents. Instead of legal forms a lawyer can be used for Estate Planning but this can be costly, take months of work, and they can make mistakes. In life people often pick a cheaper option. Importantly, often a hospital, charity, state agency, or state legislature has made a form most people use and call the "standard form", and doctors, judges, and other people may not like to follow anything else. About half this book's forms are standard forms.

PROBABLY RE-DO DOCUMENTS IF DIVORCE, MARRY, HAVE CHILD, OR MOVE

Divorcing, marrying, having a new child, or moving to a new state can have big legal effects, and if any of these events occur it is recommended people do a new Will and other Estate Planning papers soon. To help most states say a Will from another state is still valid if people move but there still can be problems.

DOCUMENTS MAY NEED TO BE WITNESSED, NOTARIZED, AND USED RIGHT

Some legal documents to be valid need to be "witnessed", which is someone watching the person doing the form sign and then the witness signs it too. Some documents need to be "notarized" where a person who is a "notary" sees a page signed and uses an ink stamp and signs too. A person who is a notary (also called a "notary public") are at some banks, brokers, insurance agents, courts, law firms, mail-copy stores, and libraries. Many people first use a phonebook to call for a notary willing to help. The words "subscribe" and "execute" means a person signed a document, and "acknowledgment" means a person said a signature was theirs. If a person signs a document in a foreign language it is usually still binding. In a form the word "respectively" means "in the order just stated". When filling out a form except for signatures the other parts can usually be done in pencil and filled in by anyone. Later people often try to keep the original pages and only hand out copies. Some people have everyone sign multiple copies to have many copies with ink signatures.

SOME LESS COMMON OR LESS USEFUL FORMS ARE NOT IN THIS BOOK

This book skips some possible but less common or less useful legal documents.

■ A "Codicil" can modify or add to a Will but it is easier and legally safer to just rewrite the whole Will.

■ Some people do a "Revocable Living Trust" so a Trust entity with a Trustee holds property or money during their life, usually done to after death have faster transfer of things and to avoid small delays, costs, or work by others (by "avoiding probate"). But this is rare as it may require moving most of a person's things to a Trust causing maybe years of hassle, mostly to avoid later small work of people happy to be getting things.

■ "Childrens Trust" papers can be done so upon a death a Trust gets things for a minor child to manage till 18, but this is rarely done due to possible costs and hassles and since it rarely matters (as this book explains).

■ A "Pet Trust" can handle money for a pet, but it's easier to just give money in a Will to person given a pet.

■ Though separate forms exist usually organ donation in handled in drivers license or state ID paperwork.

NO FEDERAL, GEORGIA, OR OTHER TAX IS USUALLY OWED AT A DEATH

Usually no tax is owed due to a death, including no estate, inheritance, death, or similar taxes.

The "Federal Estate And Gift Tax" only starts when a tax credit is used up that covers $13.61 million per person in 2024 and later (with yearly rises for inflation).

Since 2005 the state of Georgia and all local governments no longer have any estate tax or inheritance taxes that would be owed upon a death.

A few states may tax property there if the owner dies but usually only if there's over $4 million of things.

MOST WILLS HAVE A MISCELLANEOUS PART WITH HELPFUL LANGUAGE

Most Wills have a "Miscellaneous" page with legal language that might help avoid later legal problems.

INFORMATION FORM CAN HELP TELL FAMILY AND FRIENDS THINGS

Many people do some kind of "Information Form" so family or friends after a death know helpful things. People can staple financial records and other pages to this. See form on the next pages to use if wanted.

ESTATE PLANNING HELPFUL INFORMATION

For more space attach copies of form or blank pages. Keep pages by Will or other place for Executor or family.

1. Personal Information (Name, Birthdate, Social Security number, special family details, other):

2. Real estate, vehicles, and other major tangible property (especially if people may not find them):

3. Non-tangible assets like stocks, accounts, investments, loans owed you, and business interests:

4. Possible income or insurance like pensions, retirement, disability, insurance, or contracts:

5. Debts owed by you like credit card, loan, student loan, mortgage, car loans, and accounts payable:

6. Names and information of professionals used (attorneys, accountants, brokers, doctors, others):

7. Computer passwords and helpful files, document places, and safes or safe-deposit boxes code/key:

8. Other helpful things, wishes for funeral, special requests, and last messages to family and friends:

CHAPTER 2
LEGAL TERMS AND PROPERTY LAW BASICS

THERE ARE BASIC LEGAL TERMS AND IDEAS IN ESTATE PLANNING

Some legal words and ideas are basic to Estate Planning.

■ "Estate Planning" is about people doing legal documents to control things if later absent, sick, or dead. After a document is done people are mostly free to sell or transfer property, instruct doctors, or change forms.

■ A "person doing a legal document" and "doing a form" means the form is for and affects that person.

■ "Probate" is a legal process to do things after someone's death like transfer property, handle creditors, and authorize a Guardian. Due to changes in the law probate is now often informal, faster, and less costly.

■ A "Will" or "will" (this book uses upper case "W") is a legal document done to control issues after death. The phrase "Last Will And Testament" is used since a "Testament" document use to be done alongside a Will.

■ A person doing a Will is called "Testator" or "Will maker". Before about the year 2000 a woman Testator was called a "Testatrix" and woman Executor called an "Executrix" but this is no longer often said or written.

■ If no valid Will is done a person is "intestate" and then a dead person's property and money is transferred to a spouse, children, and family as intestate law says.

■ A person who died is called the "decedent" or "deceased". A person getting money or property in a Will gift is called a "recipient", "beneficiary", or "heir" if related (they "inherit"). "Survive" or "surviving" is to be alive after someone else died. The term "descendants" or "issue" usually means a person's children and grandchildren.

■ A person named in a Will to handle things after someone's death is called an "Executor", but if a judge has to pick someone they are called an "Administrator". The new term "Personal Representative" covers both these things and this new term is now very often used in Wills in Georgia and many states.

■ Legally property is: 1) "real property" which is land and buildings ("real estate"), 2) "fixtures" which are things tied to real property (like fences, carpets, and wired-in appliances), or 3) "personal property" which is everything else (like household items, clothes, tools, cars, jewelry, art, moneys, accounts, and stocks),

■ A person under 18 is usually called a "minor" and often a parent or guardian helps them do things. A minor or other person not reasonably able to make wise decisions lacks "capacity" and is "incapacitated".

■ A document giving power to someone is often called a "Power of Attorney" where the "Principal" gives power to someone called the "Agent" or "Attorney-in-Fact" (but they needn't be a real attorney or a lawyer).

■ Georgia state law is the "Official Code of Georgia" which often is in books with notes called "Annotations". State law is called the "Official Code Of Georgia Annotated" <u>or just "Georgia Code"</u>. Each small law is called a "statute" or "section" represented by a "§" symbol. A reference to a law can look like: "O. C. G. A. § 8-12-9". A legal form written in the law for people to find and use if wanted is called a "statutory form".

ESTATE MEANS PROPERTY OF DECEDENT AND ENTITY HOLDING THINGS

The "estate" or "probate estate" means <u>all property and money of a dead person</u> that at death or soon after didn't automatically legally go to new owners. Estate is also the <u>name for a temporary entity run by an Executor to do things after a death</u> (it's like a small corporation, e.g., "Estate of John Alan Smith").

PERSON CAN ONLY GIFT IN WILL WHAT THEY OWN AT DEATH

A person can often only gift by Will things they own at death, <u>so people should research what they own</u>. Basically, by law a person usually owns all they earn as wages and salary, owns their share of income and profit tied to property they own, and owns or partly owns any things their money buys or improves. And for property with "title" documents (real estate or vehicles) or where there is a "listed owner" (like accounts) the named persons are usually the legal owners unless evidence shows special circumstances. If people don't keep track of how much of their money is in an account shared with a spouse, then the account may be seen as jointly owned 50/50. Note, after doing a Will a person can sell stuff, make gifts, or transfer things, so <u>people should consider if they later transferred or lost property they named in a Will gift</u>.

NON-PROBATE TRANSFERS THAT HAPPEN AUTOMATICALLY IGNORE WILL

It is vital to be aware <u>some money or property of a person who dies may automatically transfer on death</u> or soon after to new owners <u>if certain arrangements were made earlier</u>. This is called "non-probate property". Such things transfer as arranged even if a Will names the same items in some Will gifts.

Examples are: a) a "designated beneficiary" form was done to name people to get an investment or account, b) transfer-on-death accounts were used, and c) real property is held by 2 people as "joint tenants with survivorship" or similar so at a death the surviving person gets things. Also, usually property in a Trust will ignore a Will and transfer as Trust papers say to. Life insurance usually goes to the named beneficiary.

Trying to do non-probate transfers for all things is called "avoiding probate", but few people try this since it can cause years of hassle, benefits are small, and often some thing is missed. <u>When doing a Will people should consider non-probate transfers that will occur automatically at a death and consider what will be left</u>.

THINGS OWNED IN SPECIAL WAYS MAY LIMIT GIFTING IN WILL

A person should consider if they own real estate or other property in special ownership ways which may limit gifting by Will. Laws vary in different states but <u>some common special ways of ownership are</u>:

- "joint tenant with right of survivorship" or similar legal options may be used in papers, so at a death property goes automatically to other named owners despite what a Will says (this is often how spouses hold a home);
- papers say a "life estate" exists, so then if someone dies the other people in papers the get a thing; and
- "Trust property" occurs if paperwork made a Trust entity and then property was transferred into it or this is set to occur, so then the Trust papers control where things put in the Trust go after someone's death.

Simple "joint ownership" with many owners can occur if people do joint papers, all agree to it, buy with joint funds, or if a gift was to many people. Wills <u>can</u> gift joint property, like "I give my half of boat to Ed Hu".

CHAPTER 3
WILL BASICS

WILL LETS "TESTATOR" AT LEAST AGE 14 CONTROL THINGS AFTER DEATH

A Will is a legal document done by person to control things after death, like who gets their money and property, who is Executor, who is Guardian for a child, and if faster and cheaper legal options can be used. To do a Will in Georgia a person must be at least age 14 and <u>when signing</u> be of sound mind (rational with sufficient memory) and not under duress (illegal pressure or threat). A person doing a Will is called a "Testator" or a "Will maker". When a person dies they are called the "deceased" or the "decedent".

WILL IS SIGNED BY PERSON WITH 2 OR MORE WITNESSES

WILL TO BE VALID USUALLY MUST BE SIGNED WITH 2 WITNESSES

To be a valid Will it must be written usually on paper, show it's meant as a Will, and a person must sign with 2 or more witnesses who sign too. Verbal promises about things after death are mostly not valid if not in a Will, and a "Video Will" or "Audio Will" not in writing has no power. Some people modify a Will to have 3 or 4 witnesses in case this later helps. Some other states let witnesses be skipped if a Will is handwritten.

WITNESS MUST BE AT LEAST 14 AND USUALLY NOT GETTING WILL GIFTS

<u>The 2 witnesses to a Will signing can be anyone at least age 14</u> but preferably not old or living far away. A person getting a Will gift <u>can</u> be a witness <u>but Will gifts to a witness are invalid and won't later be done</u>. Georgia Code § 53-4-20. Also in rare cases Will gifts to a spouse of a witness may raise issues with a Will. To avoid all these issues most lawyers pick witnesses so they and their spouse are not benefitting from a Will (called "disinterested" witnesses). Most lawyers also try to not use witnesses named as Executor or Guardian in a Will. Often a witness is a friend, employee at some business, stranger, or distant family.

TESTATOR AND 2 WITNESSES WHEN TOGETHER SIGN WILL

To do Will a Testator signs then usually 2 witnesses sign within minutes. Everyone should be in 1 room and see the hand of each person as they sign. The witnesses just read the 1 paragraph they sign and not the full Will. A Testator and witnesses showing others an ID is not required but usual. People need not use their full legal name if they greatly dislike it and rarely used it. Though not legally required in Georgia often a Testator says to witnesses a thing like: "My name is _____ and this is my Will I do voluntarily and I ask you 2 people to witness the signing". Some lawyers call this "publishing a Will". Some Testators also chat about a Will with witnesses to help show they know what they're doing. Often a Will has room for a witness to also print their name and address. A Testator initialing each Will page is not required but is sometimes done.

KEEP SIGNED WILL IN SAFE PLACE IT CAN BE FOUND AFTER A DEATH

People should keep Will so it can found within days of death, like in desk, drawer, safe, or less often safe deposit box. It can be given to someone to hold. It may help to tell someone where to find Will and any key. Though rarely done a person in Georgia during life can file a Will early in Probate Court for safekeeping, but if a new Will is done any old filed Will will be ignored and the old filed Will usually should be removed.

MOST WILLS SAY PEOPLE MAY LATER DO INFORMAL PROBATE

Most Wills say after a death the family and friends may do "informal probate" which can avoid costs and delays. Informal probate often is done with just 1 court hearing and often is completed in well under 1 year.

MOST WILLS SAY TO SKIP COSTLY BOND FOR EXECUTOR AND OTHERS

Most Wills helpfully say no "bond" or "surety" is required for any Executor, Guardian, or similar persons. A bond is insurance from a company to insure against misconduct. A Testator usually doesn't want a bond since the persons Testator names are trusted and them later needing a bond will cost the estate money.

CANCELING OLD WILLS IS USUALLY NOT A PROBLEM

So a new Will is followed old Wills should be canceled ("revoked"). To do this a new Will in the first part usually says old Wills are revoked. Or people can revoke a Will by marking it, like with "void" or a giant "X". Usually crossing out just part of a Will has no effect. Revoking a Will usually doesn't bring back an earlier Will.

A WILL NAMES AN EXECUTOR TO DO THINGS AFTER DEATH

A WILL NAMES SOMEONE TO BE EXECUTOR TO DO THINGS AFTER A DEATH

Usually a Will names someone as "Executor" to act after a death. The law gives Executors many helpful legal powers, like to handle debts, find and collect and give new owners property and money, and do probate If a Will fails to name an Executor a judge can pick someone, but family may argue about who to suggest. The Executor usually is not expected to use their own money to pay a dead person's debts or funeral costs. In Georgia the term "Personal Representative" and not Executor is often used for a person doing this job after a death, and these terms mostly mean the same thing. Will gifts can go to the person who is Executor.

EXECUTOR CAN BE PAID AND ESTATE PAYS FOR EXECUTOR'S EXPENSES

The law says an Executor might be paid. First, a Will can say what is the pay, like: "Executor shall be paid $3000 and no more" or "Executor shall be paid $50/hour of work and no more". Second, some people modify a Will to say an Executor should not be paid, like by writing "Executor shall not be paid including a share or percentage of property, money, and my estate". Third, if pay isn't covered in a Will the law says an Executor may get a 2.5% or a fair share of money and property in the estate. Georgia Code § 53-6-60 (b). But in most cases an Executor usually just skips asking for pay to not owe any income tax and also leave more money to later carry out Will gifts. Expenses, costs, and other needs for money of an Executor like insurance, utilities, repairs, funeral, mortgage, attorney, accountant, and probate are paid for with money or property of the estate. Any lawyer hired is usually paid whatever they and Executor agree and contract for.

EXECUTOR MUST BE AT LEAST 18 AND SECOND PERSON RARELY IS NEEDED

A person to be Executor must be at least age 18. They needn't live in Georgia but being local can help. A person can have a criminal record including a felony, but a judge may later block a person who seems too unsuitable. In a Will naming 2 people to be Executor at the same time is rare due to risk of delay arguments or delays, and since any 1 person named should be trusted. People can name a 2nd fallback person to be Executor if needed but most skip this since it is rarely needed and a judge can always just pick someone. To add such a 2nd person a Will can say: "or if they're reasonably unable to serve I name _____ to serve".

CHAPTER 4
WILL GIFTS INCLUDING RESIDUE CLAUSE

MAIN USE OF A WILL IS TO WRITE GIFTS TO HAPPEN AFTER DEATH
Most people use a Will mainly to legally say what happens to their property and money after their death, usually by writing down various Will gifts to occur when they die. Verbal and even writings about this are not usually valid if not in a written Will. A Will can control property acquired after it was signed. The end of this chapter covers "intestate law" which says where a person's things go at death if no valid Will handles this.

GIFTING IN A WILL USING SIMPLE WORDS OFTEN IS BEST
Making gifts in a Will using simple words is often best, using words like "I give to" and "I gift to". This is legally fine and avoids confusing legal words like "bequest", "devise", and "legacy" which few people know.

A PERSON IS MOSTLY FREE TO GIFT THEIR THINGS AS WANTED
A person is mostly free to give at death their money and property as they want. But creditors a decedent owed money, a spouse, and minor children under age 18 may have some rights which this book later covers.

IN WILL CAN DO SPECIFIC GIFTS TO GIFT PARTICULAR PROPERTY
Most Wills have "specific gifts" to gift <u>particular things</u>. Specific gifts can be any property, like "I give boat to Ed Blom" and "I give UBank account #84553873 to Sue Wu". If a gift is not clear the law assumes all of a kind of thing is given, like "I give jewelry to Ann Po" means <u>all</u> jewelry. But gifting specific property can have surprises like value of items can change, or a Will gift may later fail to occur if property is not owned at death.

IN WILL CAN DO GENERAL GIFTS LIKE OF MONEY
Wills can do "general gifts" where what is gifted is not particular property but can be flexibly chosen, like "I give 1 of my 3 cars to Ed Po" which lets an Executor pick which car. The usual general gift is money, like "I give $5 to Ed Hu". Money gifts are easy to write, let equal gifts be made, and are legally safer for many reasons. To carry out money gifts an Executor usually uses accounts or sells some property in the estate.

RESIDUE CLAUSE IS CATCH-ALL THAT HELPFULLY GIFTS ANYTHING LEFT
This chapter later covers how a Residue Clause in Will gifts property or money not already gifted or used.

PROPERTY OR MONEY IN A JOINT GIFT CAN GO TO MULTIPLE PEOPLE
The same property or money can go to many people to each get a part, and this is called a "joint gift". For example, "I give boat and all hats to Ann Baxter and Mary Ann Swanson" means each person owns part of every item. People later can split things by agreement or an Executor can decide how to divide items. If a person in a joint gift has died their part usually is left to transfer under a Residue Clause.

GIFT BENEFICIARIES CAN GET PERCENTAGE RATHER THAN EQUAL SHARE
If a Will gift goes to multiple people the law assumes equal shares, but if wanted percentages can be used to make unequal gifts, like "I give boat 90% to John Smith and 10% to Mary Baker".

GIFTS IN WILL CAN GO TO A CLASS OF PEOPLE

To save writing work a Will gift can go <u>to a class of people</u> like certain family or friends <u>if who is meant is later easy to determine</u>. People can <u>say roughly the total amount of money given</u> to be clearer. Examples are: "I give $10 to each member of my rock band" and "I give $10 to each grandkid so about $100 in total."

PERSON NAMED IN WILL GIFT DYING IS RARE AND MOSTLY NOT A WORRY

GIFT RECIPIENTS DYING BEFORE TESTATOR IS RARE AND USUALLY IGNORED

Having a person named to get a gift die before a Testator is <u>rare</u>. If it occurs most do nothing and trust a Residue Clause to handle it. Or some people if they notice <u>re-do a Will to replace a dead person in the Will</u>.

PERSON IN WILL GIFT <u>USUALLY</u> MUST SURVIVE OR GIFT DOES NOT OCCUR

Many Wills like this book's Will forms say a person named in a Will gift must survive (live past) the Testator for the gift to occur <u>unless gift language specifically says different</u>. If survival is not required for a Will gift then what happens if a person named in a Will gift later dies before Testator can be legally unclear. <u>People doing a Will should consider how Will gifts to people dying before Testator usually will have no effect</u>.

PEOPLE CAN ADD AN ALTERNATE BENEFICIARY LIKE FOR SPECIAL ITEMS

Some people for the small risk a recipient in a Will gift dies before Testator, and maybe for special items, <u>add a bit to put an "alternate beneficiary"</u>, like "I give boat to Ed Fox but if they don't survive me to Ann Fox".

IF PERSON IN WILL GIFT DIES <u>IT CAN INSTEAD GO TO "LINEAL DESCENDANTS"</u>

A Will gift can say it goes to a person but in the rare chance they don't survive (live past the Testator) then to their "lineal descendants per stirpes". <u>Descendants are a person's children and grandchildren</u>. Often a Residue Clause uses "lineal descendants" wording. Also, the term "per stirpes" is often used which basically means give to each family branch equally. <u>An example shows how "lineal descendants" wording works</u>:

A Will may say: "All clothes to Sue Wu but if they don't survive to their lineal descendants per stirpes", and this means if Sue Wu has died and her son Ken Wu is living and her other son Ben Wu has died but left 2 children then, legally, by law Ken Wu himself gets 50% and Ben Wu's 2 children each get 25%.

CAN LEAVE SOME WILL GIFT AREAS BLANK OR WRITE TO SAY SKIP GIFTS

A person can choose to not use some gifts areas in a Will legal form, like by just leaving areas blank, writing things like "SKIPPED" or "NONE", or using a computer to delete some gift lines. Judges and others usually do not care about neatness or empty spaces in Wills, and will follow whatever parts are filled in.

FAMILIES MAY LET PEOPLE TAKE ITEMS MENTIONED IN NOTES OR STICKERS

Many families let people take items <u>unofficially</u> in ways a person before they died mentioned, wrote on notes, or showed by stickers. If anyone objects a judge will have a Will and law be fully followed, but later people can voluntarily retransfer items. <u>This book also covers the "Gift List" form that can say who should get items</u>.

RESIDUE CLAUSE GIFTING ANYTHING LEFT IS MAIN WAY TO GIFT THINGS

THE RESIDUE CLAUSE IS A CATCH-ALL THAT GIFTS ANYTHING LEFT

Most Wills by the end have a Residue Clause to give property or money left in a person's estate not gifted earlier in a Will or used other ways. All that is left this way is called the "Residue". Many people let this clause handle most things. This avoids all need to list and describe property and money and also has less legal risk.

USUAL RESIDUE CLAUSE HAS 2 PARTS

A 2 part Residue Clause with "lineal descendants" language is usual (see this book's previous page), with:

1) a 1st space to name persons to get things if they survive the Testator (many name a spouse or closest family here), and if several people are named here but only some survive the survivors split things, and

2) a 2nd space to name persons to get things if all in the 1st space don't survive (many people name next closest family or friends here), and if anyone in the 2nd space has died their lineal descendants get their part.

EXAMPLE OF 2 PART RESIDUE CLAUSE

"RESIDUE CLAUSE: The rest, residue, and remainder of my estate, and anything else, I give to:

a) to ____Jay Doe my husband_____ who survive me and with persons just named who survive me taking the share of non-survivors, then if anything remains

b) to ____Sam Doe, Ann Wu, and Pam Ax_____ and if any of those just named do not survive me their part goes to their lineal descendants per stirpes."

In this example things may go to "descendants" so to a person's children and grandchildren, and things may be divided "per stirpes" which means equal among family branches. In this example if Jay Doe has survived he gets everything. If he has died and also Sam Doe hasn't survived but he left 2 children then, legally, Sam's 2 children split the 1/3 share of his (so get 1/6 each) and the other 2 persons in 2nd part (Ann Wu and Pam Ax) get 1/3 each. Usually the first people named in the clause won't die so gets things.

SOME PEOPLE WRITE THE SAME THING IN BOTH PARTS OR SKIP A PART

Some people put the same names in both clause spaces or skip part of it to do certain things. For example, a person with no spouse may skip the 1st part and in 2nd part name their children (including any who died who had kids of their own) so all branches of a person's descendants get a share. *See example in Appendix.*

SOME PEOPLE USE PERCENTAGES TO GIFT DIFFERENT AMOUNTS OF RESIDUE

Some people use percentages in a Residue Clause to get the exact split wanted. This can be used to gift a lot (like to a person's children) and gift a small bit (like to more distant people). *See example in Appendix.*

SOME PEOPLE CHANGE A RESIDUE CLAUSE TO HAVE 1 PART

Some people change a Residue Clause to have just 1 part since this can gift more equally and be easier to understand. *See example in Appendix.* For example a Residue Clause can be made to say:

"The rest, residue, and remainder of my estate, and anything else, I give to _____ who survive me and if any of those just named do not survive me their part goes to their lineal descendants per stirpes."

MUST SUFFICIENTLY DESCRIBE NAMES AND PROPERTY IN A WILL

PUTTING NAMES OF PEOPLE OR GROUPS IN A WILL IS FAIRLY EASY

Putting names in a Will is fairly easy. <u>Later a judge or Executor assume a person putting names in a Will meant to gift to people they know, so common names are OK unless 2 friends or family use the same name</u>. Details can help if names won't be recognized or to be friendly, like "I give $5 to my nurse Sue Smith" and "I give $5 to loyal pal Ed Dutton". If people mostly used a nickname "also known as" or "a/k/a" may help, like "I give $5 to Dan Smith a/k/a Big Red". Gifts can go to a charity, a government, or a group, like "I give $8 to Goodwill Charities, "I give $8 to the Gwinnett County Library in Georgia", and "I give $8 to Sacred Trinity Church of Dallas, Texas". People sometimes phone to learn a charity's or organization's official name.

PUTTING DESCRIPTIONS OF ITEMS IN WILL GIFTS IS FAIRLY EASY

Describing items in gifts is fairly easy. <u>Later a judge or Executor assume a person in a Will meant to gift items they own, and rarely do people own similar things so there is later confusion</u>. Often OK is doing gifts with simple words like: "I give ax to Ed Wu" and "I give big table to Jed Fox". It's OK to gift by category or a list, like: "I give tools to Sam Lee" and "I give cow, van, and harp to Sue Hill". For financial items plain words can be used, like "I give bank accounts and stocks to Ann Wu", or details can be used, like: "I give Citigroup bank account ending in 8714 to Tom Hud". <u>Gifting using a location is riskier</u> as judges will ignore a Will gift if it seems items were placed to affect gifting and for no "independently significant" life reason. So, "I give Ed Po items in my desk and safe" a judge might not follow, but "I give Ed Po hats at cabin" likely is OK.

DESCRIBING REAL PROPERTY IS HARD IF NOT USING RESIDUE OR TITLE

Gifting real property (real estate) and fixtures (things tied to real property like fences, furnaces, and wiring) at death can be hard to do right and the legally safer way to do this is:

a) <u>do nothing specific so it's handled by a Will residue clause</u>, or b) <u>have a lawyer or other person put names in a deed or other document for the real property</u> so then named persons legally get it when the owner dies.

Gifting real property at death a few other ways is legally harder. Helpfully a gift of real property <u>using a location</u> by law gifts <u>all land, buildings, and fixtures located there</u> with no need to list out what's there.

It is possible to <u>gift real property at a particular address with very plain words</u>, like a house, fixtures, and land can be fully given by something like: "I give 86 Hart Street, Atlanta, Georgia, to Sue Ann Brown".

People can do a <u>blanket gift</u> giving all of a kind of property, like, "I give all real property and fixtures in Fulton County, Georgia to Ann Ivy Hill " or "I give all real property and fixtures of mine anywhere to Mary Sue Fox".

Giving real property in a Will using a "legal description" is how some lawyers do it, but this can be hard to do. If using a legal description people must write without mistakes <u>the full legal description of maybe many lines</u> into a Will with no abbreviation at all. A legal description might be found on a deed or on mortgage papers. Legal descriptions may refer to a "lot" or "blocks" on a map which is recorded in land records of a county, or it may refer to a path around the land borders with various angles, distances, and iron stakes.

AT START OF MOST WILLS PEOPLE NAME ANY SPOUSE AND CHILDREN

Most Wills <u>start with a spot to write names of current living spouse and children of any age</u>. This book's Will forms do this. Natural or adopted children should be put here even if born outside of marriage (but not any stepchildren). People without this family can skip this part or write a thing like "none". Not writing down this family may invalidate a Will by indicating a person is mentally unfit, or let the family not listed <u>ask a judge to give them more or all</u> money and property by claiming they were skipped due to a writing mistake or brief loss of memory. After listing any spouse and children a Testator is mostly allowed to not give them anything.

PUTTING CONDITIONS ON WILL GIFTS IS RARE DUE TO POSSIBLE PROBLEMS

Putting conditions on a gift, like "I give Ann Poe $90 if she graduates college", can cause problems like years of delay, risk of lawsuits, and big attorney's fees. Due to all this conditions are rarely put on Will gifts.

MOST STATES AND WILLS SAY PEOPLE TO GET GIFTS MUST SURVIVE 5 DAYS

Helpful laws in most states and all this book's Will forms say if a person dies within 5 days (120 hours) of a Testator or simultaneously, then they are legally seen as dying before the Testator. This skips the need to prove exact time of death (like if people die in 1 accident), and avoids a Will gift or right to something going to someone who then soon dies within days (so an item may have to go through multiple probate proceedings).

LATER DIVORCE OR MURDER CANCELS WILL GIFTS TO THE ACTING PERSON

If a person divorces or murders a Testator then <u>by state law</u> usually all Will gifts to them are cancelled.

MOST WILLS HAVE A MISCELLANEOUS PART WITH HELPFUL LANGUAGE

Most Wills have a "Miscellaneous" page with legal language that might help avoid later legal problems.

INTESTATE LAW COVERS PROPERTY OR MONEY NOT HANDLED BY WILL

State "intestate law" says <u>if a person dies with no valid Will</u> or <u>if anything is left after Will and other transfers are done</u> then certain surviving (living) family get property and money left in a person's estate. Note, "descendants" and "issue" mean a person's children and grandchildren, and if a person dies who'd have got an intestate share often their closest descendants legally get that share. Many people like how intestate law divides things and choose to skip a Will, but often doing a Will can avoid costs and delays. State intestate law if it applies, which is <u>mostly at Georgia Code § 53-2-1 (c)</u>, says roughly <u>in order</u>:

1. If you die with living descendants but no spouse, the closest descendants get things (including money);
2. If you die with a living spouse but no descendants, the spouse get things;
3. If you die with both living spouse and living descendants, the spouse and descendants equally share things (but the spouse may not get less than 1/3);
4. If you die with living parents but no spouse or descendants, the parents get things;
5. If you die with living brothers or sisters but no spouse or descendants or parents, the siblings get things;
6. If you die with none of the above family still living, then the other close family get things; and
7. If none of the above persons are living when a Testator dies, then the state of Georgia gets things.

CHAPTER 5
DEBT, MARRIAGE, AND YOUNG CHILD ISSUES

THIS CHAPTER IS ABOUT COMPLEX ISSUES IT MAY HELP TO LEARN ABOUT
This chapter is about some complex issues some people face. People who want can do more research.

DEBT ISSUES

PAYING DECEDENT'S DEBTS MAY USE UP RESOURCES AND REDUCE GIFTS
Creditors owed by a decedent can ask a judge to be paid from decedent's money and property before Will gifts are carried out. But if decedent didn't have much money and property at death then the creditors often don't bother, for reasons said below. Resources to pay debts first come from things in Will Residue, then Will general gifts like of money, and then Will specific gifts. Some debts like for probate, attorney, funeral, and health care have priority to be paid first. Helpfully a spouse and family aren't usually personally liable to pay decedent's debts for non-necessities unless they guaranteed or co-signed the particular loans. People should consider how paying debts may use up money or property leaving less to carry out Will gifts.

BEFORE DEBTS ARE PAID MAY COME FAMILY RIGHTS IN SOME STATES
Most states say a spouse or minor children have "family rights" they can ask to get before debts are paid, which can help family get something even if decedent had big debts. Many states say family may claim things like a "year living allowance", a small share of decedent's things as "exempt property", and a few other rights. Family rights use up money and property so if used less may be left to do Will gifts. Creditors know of family rights so often don't bother to seek payment if told decedent had little wealth, and if their phone calls are ignored by family. Georgia is a bit unique and only has a "Year's Support" as a family right, but this might be calculated using the full yearly income of the decedent to give quite a lot to family leaving little for creditors. People if they want can research state law.

HOMESTEAD LAWS MAY PROTECT HOME FOR FAMILY IN SOME STATES
"Homestead" laws in some states say a decedent's creditors can't seek payment by foreclosing or selling a decedent's house if their spouse or children under 18 are living there (unless equity is big, like $400,000). Also, homestead laws often say a spouse or minor children get ownership of decedent's house (or a right to occupy it for their life in some states) if the decedent owned it and despite a Will gift giving it to other people. Georgia is unusual without most of these laws but often in Georgia a spouse or minor children can ask to live in a house while probate occurs or a fair time which can be year or more. Due to all these factors and to help their family most people give spouse or if no spouse the minor children a house by Will or putting them on title. Of course a normal mortgage later can be foreclosed if not paid monthly. People can research state law.

USUALLY SECURED DEBTS LIKE MORTGAGE OR VEHICLE LIEN NOT PAID OFF
Most states have laws saying secured debts like house mortgage or car lien are not paid off after a death but remain even if a Will says generally to pay debts. This book's Wills say don't pay such debts unless a person writes in Will to do so. This avoids using up much money and property so little is left to do Will gifts. Later if a mortgage or lien remains and is not paid monthly then foreclosure or repossession may occur.

If a person wants at death to pay off secured debts either: a) they can in a Will give a person getting property enough cash to pay off the debt, or b) write an order to pay in Will (like "I order mortgage on cabin paid off"). People who get a house, car, or other thing with a lien or mortgage must usually later pay monthly payments to avoid foreclosure or repossession.

MARRIAGE ISSUES

MOST STATES USE "SEPARATE PROPERTY LAW" FOR SPOUSES

Most states including Georgia use "Separate Property" law saying married person mostly owns money and property separately, and usually owns their own income, profits, and accounts and property in their name. Due to this a spouse is mostly free to sell during life their things, or gift in their Will their things even acting alone without their spouse. But joint ownership by 2 spouses can arise by normal ways (like by agreement, paying half a purchase price, and also many spouses do paperwork to own a house jointly).

"COMMUNITY PROPERTY" LAW APPLIES IN OTHER STATES FOR SPOUSES

There are 9 states mostly in West and South U.S.A. that use "Community Property" law for spouses. This says if a married person lives in these states most property or money gotten is usually owned 50/50 by spouses as "Community Property" if it relates to activities during a marriage (like from labor or wages, or active management of a small business) or if bought or improved with other Community Property. Community Property law states are Arizona, California, Louisiana, Idaho, Nevada, New Mexico, Texas, Washington, and Wisconsin. People in Georgia avoid these issues unless they have very recently moved.

SPOUSE CAN SEEK "ELECTIVE SHARE" IN SOME STATES

Many states so a surviving spouse has enough to live on gives them if unhappy a right to not take what a Will gifts them and instead choose (elect) an "Elective Share" of the dead spouse's property and money. Many states say the Elective Share is half, or says it starts at 15% rising to 50% with length of marriage. Georgia is unique in not having an Elective Share, but it does give a spouse a right to "Year's Support" during probate from the dead spouse's money and property which to help is often set generously as the dead spouse's salary. Also, a spouse may have made promises which in rare cases may support a later lawsuit, like "take care of me through my major illness despite the huge hardship and in return you'll get the house and half of all I have". Because of all this a married person often gifts by Will and other ways mostly to a spouse (like at least 50% and family house) to avoid a spouse being upset or trying to do other actions.

YOUNG CHILD ISSUES

WILL CAN NAME A "GUARDIAN" TO GIVE PERSONAL CARE TO YOUNG CHILD

If a parent dies with a child under age 18 then any other natural or adopted parent (but not a step-parent) usually automatically gets control of the child's personal care (including health care, school, and home issues). This won't occur only if the 2nd parent will be unavailable a long time, or is proven unfit in court, which is rare. But just in case it's ever needed (like later both parents die) a Will often names a healthy willing relative or friend as "Guardian" to if needed give this care for a child. Some states call this a "Guardian Of The Person".

WILL CAN NAME "CONSERVATOR" TO WATCH CHILD'S PROPERTY AND MONEY

Since a child until age 18 can't legally easily control property and money a Will often names a person to have the job of managing property and money a child has or may get. This person decides each year how to use property and money on a child's needs (like on school, health care, and living costs) and then usually at age 18 anything left then goes to the child. In Georgia this person is called a "Conservator". Some states call this a "Guardian Of The Estate" or a "Guardian Of Property". Any person who paid things to help a child especially in the first months after a parent's death can ask the Conservator to pay them back these costs. Note, as a nice 2nd option to avoid legal work and costs most Wills say an Executor may also name a person as "Custodian" to handle a child's property and money under the Uniform Transfers To Minors Act.

MOST WILLS NAME 1 PERSON TO CARE FOR CHILD AND THEIR PROPERTY

This book's Will forms and most parents name the same 1 person to care for a child and also manage a child's property and money. People can change a Will to name different people for the 2 positions, but this is rarely worth it since parents dying is rare, rarely do children get much, a person smart enough to handle a child often can handle money, and naming different people can lead to arguments and even costly lawsuits between people. Will gifts can go to someone named to be a Guardian or Conservator.

PERSON TO HELP A CHILD MUST BE AT LEAST 18

To be a person helping a child in Georgia a person must be at least age 18 but they needn't reside here. But later usually a judge can't think they are clearly unfit to serve, which usually means no serious criminal felony or a history of abuse or fraud. The choice by the last living parent is usually followed. If no Will names a person for a position or they're unavailable a judge can pick someone, but family may argue about this. Naming 2 people to act at the same time in the same position is rare since 2 persons may argue and any 1 person named should be smart enough to act alone. In rare cases a married couple is named for the same position but there can be problems if they divorce or disagree. Some Wills add a 2nd person to serve if the 1st person named is later not available, like: "or if they are later unable to serve I name _____ to serve"). But most people skip naming a fallback person since it is rarely needed, if a problem is seen a Will can be redone by a person, and a judge can just pick someone if needed.

NAMING PERSONS TO HELP CHILD RARELY MATTERS

A child under 18 having parents die is rare so parents shouldn't worry much about naming people to help. A good U.S. study looked at 72,240 people under age 18 and found only 2014 had lost 1 parent (so 2.78%) and only 97 had lost 2 parents (so a very small 0.13%). *Parent Mortality Census SIPP Paper #288.*

CHAPTER 6
BASIC IDEAS ABOUT HEALTH CARE FORMS

BASIC IDEAS HELP PEOPLE UNDERSTAND CONTROLLING HEALTH CARE

Some ideas help people understand health care forms.

■ By law people controls their own health care by telling medical personnel what they want <u>unless they are "incapacitated"</u> by insufficient ability to a) <u>communicate</u> verbally or by notes, b) be <u>rational</u>, or c) be <u>conscious</u>. Most people keep control of their own care till death or till no big treatment options remain, but some people worry they may be incapacitated a long time so want to do health care forms.

■ Legal documents that help control health care are usually called "Advanced Directives".

■ If an adult 18 or older becomes incapacitated <u>the adult's closest family like spouse or adult child usually can make emergency decisions</u>. But later they usually must then rush to a judge to get further power if no legal document gives them more power over health care.

■ In legal documents a <u>person can be named to have control of health care</u> if needed. This person is often called the "Health Care Agent" or similar.

■ In legal documents people can give <u>written medical instructions that doctors, family, and Agent must obey</u>.

■ Parents even without legal documents usually have power over health care of <u>children under age 18</u>.

■ Some <u>married people</u> do documents to give a spouse power over medical care if they are incapacitated. Some adults give this power to parents. Young people are rarely badly sick so often skip doing these things.

■ Pain relief like pain drugs or comfort care is still given even if documents say to stop or limit other care.

■ <u>Most people only do 1 legal document</u> about health care that often names someone to control health care if needed and has a spot for basic instructions (this is sometimes called a "Health Care Power of Attorney").

■ For the rare times stopping health care seems more likely to matter (like due to extreme illness or old age):

-- most people do nothing special and trust family or Health Care Agent to wisely decide when to stop care (they can weigh many factors like pain, cost, likely difficulty of treatment, beliefs, and chances of recovery);

-- a few people do a serious document to say to stop most health care if <u>later</u> doctors think an incapacitated person has very bad health and more medical care likely won't help (sometimes this is called a "Living Will";

-- a few people do a serious document to say <u>starting immediately</u> to not give most medical care (often this is called a "Do-Not-Resuscitate" if about resuscitation, or called a "Physician's Order" if about many treatments).

CHAPTER 7
FORM 1: WILL (STANDARD)

FORM 1 IS A STANDARD WILL THAT IS FLEXIBLE BUT WITHOUT GUARDIAN

Form 1 is a flexible Will that lets a person control many things after their death. This form has no part about a Guardian so is for a person with no child under age 18. A person doing a Will is called a Testator.

FORM IS A WILL WITH SEVERAL PARTS

The form starts with lines for a person to put their name (a full legal name is best but not required) and place of main residence (most put a county but some put a city). The Will is still valid if people later move.

Paragraph 1, "Living Spouse And Children", is used to write names of any living spouse and living children (but not step-children) of any age (or if there are none skip this or maybe put "none"). This helps show a person is mentally fit enough to do a Will. Wrongly not listing someone may cause legal problems.

Paragraph 2, "Gifts", has many spaces to make some specific gifts of particular property or some general gifts like of money. People can delete, copy and paste to add more, or leave blank these gift lines.

Paragraph 3, "Separate Writings", says to follow any separate writings done apart from the Will that gifts tangible personal property in manner allowed by state law.

Paragraph 4, "Residue", has a Residue Clause to say any property and money left after earlier Will parts and other transfers is to be distributed in the way a person wrote in the blank parts of this paragraph.

Paragraph 5, "Administration", names a person to be Personal Representative to do things after a person's death (in the past the term Executor was usually used in Georgia for the person doing this job).

Paragraph 6, "Miscellaneous", has paragraphs of legal language to help avoid certain legal issues.

Last is a paragraph for Testator to put the date and sign, and a paragraph for 2 witnesses to put the date, sign, and print the addresses they live at.

USUAL RESIDUE CLAUSE HAS 2 PLACES TO NAME PERSONS TO GET THINGS

In a Will "Residue Clause" anything left over after other Will parts is transferred as the clause directs. Many people use a Residue Clause to gift most their things. In this Will form's Residue Clause there is:

1) a 1st space to name 1 or more persons to get the Residue, and if any named here have died before the Will maker then other persons named here in this 1st space take the dead person's share, and

2) a 2nd space to name people to get things if all people named in the 1st space have died, and if any people named in the 2nd space have died their shares go to "lineal descendants" like their children.

People often put in the 1st space a spouse or closest family or friends, and in 2nd space next closest people.

TESTATOR AND 2 WITNESSES WHILE TOGETHER SIGN WILL

This Will after being filled out (except bits intentionally left blank) must be signed by the person doing the Will (the "Testator") in front of at least 2 persons acting as witnesses at least age 18 who then also sign.

LAST WILL AND TESTAMENT

I, _____, of _____, Georgia, do revoke all prior Wills and testamentary documents and do make, publish, and declare this as my Will. I am of sound mind and under no duress or undue influence and act voluntarily.

1. LIVING SPOUSE AND CHILDREN. To show I am mentally fit and have sufficient memory to do a Will I say I now have the following living spouse and living children:
_____
_____.

2. GIFTS. I give these gifts in this Will, but to get a gift in this section the recipient must survive me except as otherwise stated below.

I give _____ to _____.
I give _____ to _____.
I give _____ to _____.
I give _____ to _____.
I give _____ to _____.
I give _____ to _____.
I give _____ to _____.
I give _____ to _____.
I give _____ to _____.
I give _____ to _____.
I give _____ to _____.
I give _____ to _____.

3. SEPARATE WRITINGS. I may do writings separate from this Will to gift tangible personal property as allowed by state law, and all such writings should be followed. But any such writing not found within 90 days of my death is canceled and has no effect. A gift in such a writing to a person who does not survive me is canceled and has no effect. This Will does not revoke any such writings that now exist.

4. RESIDUE. The rest, residue, and remainder of my estate, and anything else, I give:
   a) to _____ who survive me, and with persons just named who survive me taking the share of non-survivors, then if anything remains
   b) to _____ and if any of those just now named do not survive me their part goes to their lineal descendants per stirpes.

5. ADMINISTRATION. I name, nominate, and appoint _____ as Personal Representative including for me, my Will, and my estate.

6. MISCELLANEOUS. The following applies to this Will and generally.
   In this Will no part left unfilled is a mistake including spaces in the residue clause.
   The facts support and I want Georgia state law to apply to this Will and my estate.
   I order that my just debts, funeral and related expenses, and taxes be paid as soon after my death as practical but only those items my Personal Representative chooses to pay.
   Any gift of money in this Will has priority over gifts in any separate writing.
   Priority of Will gifts of the same type is based on the order they are made in this Will.
   The words give and gift also means a devise, bequest, grant, legacy, or similar.
   I am intentionally not providing by Will or other ways for some family, including I am not providing for some children of mine and also children of a deceased child of mine.
   If a Will gift reasonably mentions survival then survival is an absolute condition and anti-lapse laws or similar provisions have no effect and without survival the gift lapses. Unless a Will gift specifies otherwise if a Will gift goes to multiple recipients if any do not survive me the part to them lapses and instead goes to other surviving recipients.
   No earlier transfer reduces a Will gift unless I usually called it a loan or advancement.
   In this Will any gendered word includes all genders, and the singular includes the plural and vice versa, and the word "they" can mean a single person or many persons.
   Unless a Will specifically says otherwise a secured debt including a mortgage or lien shall not be paid off including by a Personal Representative or in probate, and a recipient of a Will gift of property takes it subject to debts. Also, no recipient of property who may lose it or who pays to keep it may have my estate or other people pay or do exoneration.
   If I lost or no longer have an item in a Will specific gift then the gift is extinguished.
   I request and authorize any informal, summary, and quick probate or similar action. Any Personal Representative may act independently with no supervision of any court, including independent administration, and with no inventory, appraisal, or other action.
   I give any Personal Representative power to lease, sell, mortgage, convey, or keep property including real property in a manner and time they deem helpful or proper.
I give any Personal Representative authority to settle or pay claims or debts in the time and manner they choose. I give any Personal Representative all powers and authority that may be given by statute or common law in any jurisdiction, including powers and authorities conferred by the Georgia Revised Probate Code of 1998 and Revised Georgia Trust Code

of 2010, as amended, plus Georgia Code §§ 53-12-261 and 263 et seq., as amended.

Any Guardian of any type, Conservator, Custodian, or other person managing a minor's property or money may use or invade the principal and sell property without court action.

If context permits the terms Personal Representative and Executor and Administrator are interchangeable, Conservator and Guardian of the Estate and Guardian of Property and Custodian are interchangeable, and residue and residuary are interchangeable. Any such person may stand in the place of and have all powers like the others named here.

The residue includes lapsed or failed gifts, insurance paid to the estate, digital assets, inheritances owed me, and all I had power of appointment or testamentary disposition over.

Any Personal Representative may access, manage, delete, modify, transfer, and otherwise control any digital accounts and assets I had any interest in or power over.

Any Personal Representative, Executor, Administrator, Guardian of any type like for a person or estate, Conservator, Custodian, and any other fiduciary under this Will or otherwise shall qualify and serve without bond, surety, security, surety bond, or similar.

If evidence does not show it likely a person survived me by 120 hours (5 days) then for this Will and my estate they shall be deemed in all ways as having died before me.

Any Personal Representative may at any time transfer money or property of a minor under age 18 to a Custodian to act under the Georgia Uniform Transfers to Minors Act or similar law anywhere, and may pick a person to be Custodian including themselves.

If part of this Will is invalid or unenforceable other provisions shall remain in effect.

TESTATOR

IN WITNESS WHEREOF and in the presence of two witnesses, who are acting as witnesses at my request, in my presence and in the presence of each other, I hereunto sign my name on the _____ day of _____, 20_____.

_____
Signature of Testator

WITNESSES

The foregoing instrument was signed by the Testator in our presence and declared by the Testator to be the Testator's Will, and we, the undersigned witnesses, sign our names hereunto as witnesses at the request and in the presence of the Testator, and in the presence of each other on the _____ day of _____, 20_____.

_____   _____
Signature of Witness   Address of Witness

_____   _____
Signature of Witness   Address of Witness

CHAPTER 8
FORM 2: WILL (GUARDIAN)

FORM 2 IS A WILL WITH GUARDIAN PART FOR A PERSON WITH YOUNG CHILD
Form 2 is a Will with a Guardian part to be used by a person with a minor child under age 18.

FORM IS A WILL WITH SEVERAL PARTS INCLUDING A GUARDIAN PART
The form starts with lines for a person to put their name (a full legal name is best but not required) and place of main residence (most put a county but some put a city). The Will is still valid if people later move.

Paragraph 1, "Living Spouse And Children", is used to write names of any living spouse and living children (but not step-children) of any age (or if there are none skip this or maybe put "none"). This helps show a person is mentally fit enough to do a Will. Wrongly not listing someone may cause legal problems.

Paragraph 2, "Gifts", has many spaces to make some specific gifts of particular property or some general gifts like of money. People can delete, copy and paste to add more, or leave blank these gift lines.

Paragraph 3, "Separate Writings", says to follow any separate writings done apart from the Will that gifts tangible personal property in manner allowed by state law.

Paragraph 4, "Residue", has a Residue Clause to say any property and money left after earlier Will parts and other transfers is to be distributed in the way a person wrote in the blank parts of this paragraph.

Paragraph 5, "Administration", names a person to be Personal Representative to do things after a person's death (in the past the term Executor was usually used in Georgia for the person doing this job).

<u>**Paragraph 6, "Guardian"** lets a person be named as "Guardian" to care for a child under 18 if needed (life if both parents die) and be named as "Conservator" to manage property and money of any young child</u>.

Paragraph 7, "Miscellaneous", has paragraphs of legal language to help avoid certain legal issues.

Last is a paragraph for Testator and 2 witnesses to put some dates, names, addresses.

USUAL RESIDUE CLAUSE HAS 2 PLACES TO NAME PERSONS TO GET THINGS
In a Will "Residue Clause" anything left over after other Will parts is transferred as the clause directs. Many people use a Residue Clause to gift most their things. In this Will form's Residue Clause there is:

1) a 1st space to name 1 or more persons to get the Residue, and if any named here have died before the Will maker then other persons named here in this 1st space take the dead person's share, and

2) a 2nd space to name people to get things if all people named in the 1st space have died, and if any people named in the 2nd space have died their shares go to "lineal descendants" like their children.

People often put in the 1st space a spouse or closest family or friends, and in 2nd space next closest people.

TESTATOR AND 2 WITNESSES WHILE TOGETHER SIGN WILL
This Will after being filled out (except bits intentionally left blank) must be signed by the person doing the Will (the "Testator") in front of at least 2 persons acting as witnesses at least age 18 who then also sign.

LAST WILL AND TESTAMENT

I, _____, of _____, Georgia, do revoke all prior Wills and testamentary documents and do make, publish, and declare this as my Will. I am of sound mind and under no duress or undue influence and act voluntarily.

1. LIVING SPOUSE AND CHILDREN. To show I am mentally fit and have sufficient memory to do a Will I say I now have the following living spouse and living children:
_____
_____.

2. GIFTS. I give these gifts in this Will, but to get a gift in this section the recipient must survive me except as otherwise stated below.

I give _____ to _____.
I give _____ to _____.
I give _____ to _____.
I give _____ to _____.
I give _____ to _____.
I give _____ to _____.
I give _____ to _____.
I give _____ to _____.
I give _____ to _____.

3. SEPARATE WRITINGS. I may do writings separate from this Will to gift tangible personal property as allowed by state law, and all such writings should be followed. But any such writing not found within 90 days of my death is canceled and has no effect. A gift in such a writing to a person who does not survive me is canceled and has no effect. This Will does not revoke any such writings that now exist.

4. RESIDUE. The rest, residue, and remainder of my estate, and anything else, I give:
   a) to _____ who survive me, and with persons just named who survive me taking the share of non-survivors, then if anything remains
   b) to _____ and if any of those just now named do not survive me their part goes to their lineal descendants per stirpes.

5. ADMINISTRATION. I name, nominate, and appoint _____
as Personal Representative including for me, my Will, and my estate.

6. GUARDIAN. I name _____ to be Guardian of any minor child of mine and also to have care, authority, custody, and other control of them (including as Guardian Of The Person). I also name this same person to be Conservator for any minor child and also to have care, control, and power over their property, money, and estate.

7. MISCELLANEOUS. The following applies to this Will and generally.

In this Will no part left unfilled is a mistake including spaces in the residue clause.
The facts support and I want Georgia state law to apply to this Will and my estate.
I order that my just debts, funeral and related expenses, and taxes be paid as soon after my death as practical but only those items my Personal Representative chooses to pay.
Any gift of money in this Will has priority over gifts in any separate writing.
Priority of Will gifts of the same type is based on the order they are made in this Will.
The words give and gift also means a devise, bequest, grant, legacy, or similar.
I am intentionally not providing by Will or other ways for some family, including I am not providing for some children of mine and also children of a deceased child of mine.
If a Will gift reasonably mentions survival then survival is an absolute condition and anti-lapse laws or similar provisions have no effect and without survival the gift lapses. Unless a Will gift specifies otherwise if a Will gift goes to multiple recipients if any do not survive me the part to them lapses and instead goes to other surviving recipients.
No earlier transfer reduces a Will gift unless I usually called it a loan or advancement.
In this Will any gendered word includes all genders, and the singular includes the plural and vice versa, and the word "they" can mean a single person or many persons.
Unless a Will specifically says otherwise a secured debt including a mortgage or lien shall not be paid off including by a Personal Representative or in probate, and a recipient of a Will gift of property takes it subject to debts. Also, no recipient of property who may lose it or who pays to keep it may have my estate or other people pay or do exoneration.
If I lost or no longer have an item in a Will specific gift then the gift is extinguished.
I request and authorize any informal, summary, and quick probate or similar action. Any Personal Representative may act independently with no supervision of any court, including independent administration, and with no inventory, appraisal, or other action.
I give any Personal Representative power to lease, sell, mortgage, convey, or keep property including real property in a manner and time they deem helpful or proper.
I give any Personal Representative authority to settle or pay claims or debts in the time and manner they choose. I give any Personal Representative all powers and authority that may be given by statute or common law in any jurisdiction, including powers and authorities conferred by the Georgia Revised Probate Code of 1998 and Revised Georgia Trust Code of 2010, as amended, plus Georgia Code §§ 53-12-261 and 263 et seq., as amended.

Any Guardian of any type, Conservator, Custodian, or other person managing a minor's property or money may use or invade the principal and sell property without court action.

If context permits the terms Personal Representative and Executor and Administrator are interchangeable, Conservator and Guardian of the Estate and Guardian of Property and Custodian are interchangeable, and residue and residuary are interchangeable. Any such person may stand in the place of and have all powers like the others named here.

The residue includes lapsed or failed gifts, insurance paid to the estate, digital assets, inheritances owed me, and all I had power of appointment or testamentary disposition over.

Any Personal Representative may access, manage, delete, modify, transfer, and otherwise control any digital accounts and assets I had any interest in or power over.

Any Personal Representative, Executor, Administrator, Guardian of any type like for a person or estate, Conservator, Custodian, and any other fiduciary under this Will or otherwise shall qualify and serve without bond, surety, security, surety bond, or similar.

If evidence does not show it likely a person survived me by 120 hours (5 days) then for this Will and my estate they shall be deemed in all ways as having died before me.

Any Personal Representative may at any time transfer money or property of a minor under age 18 to a Custodian to act under the Georgia Uniform Transfers to Minors Act or similar law anywhere, and may pick a person to be Custodian including themselves.

If part of this Will is invalid or unenforceable other provisions shall remain in effect.

TESTATOR

IN WITNESS WHEREOF and in the presence of two witnesses, who are acting as witnesses at my request, in my presence and in the presence of each other, I hereunto sign my name on the _____ day of _____, 20_____.

_____
Signature of Testator

WITNESSES

The foregoing instrument was signed by the Testator in our presence and declared by the Testator to be the Testator's Will, and we, the undersigned witnesses, sign our names hereunto as witnesses at the request and in the presence of the Testator, and in the presence of each other on the _____ day of _____, 20_____.

_____   _____
Signature of Witness   Address of Witness

_____   _____
Signature of Witness   Address of Witness

CHAPTER 9
FORM 3: SELF-PROVING AFFIDAVIT

FORM CAN BE DONE TO HELP WITH THE WORK OF USING A WILL LATER

This Self-Proving Affidavit form is optional but can be done anytime after a Will is done to help a bit with legal work involved in later using a Will after a death. This chapter's form is <u>copied exactly from the statutory form</u> found in law at Georgia Code § 53-4-24.

FORM HELPS SHOW A WILL WAS PROPERLY SIGNED

The Self-Proving Affidavit helps "prove" a Will was signed properly. If this form isn't done then after a death a little more work is needed to get evidence from either witnesses to the Will signing, persons familiar with signatures of people, or a handwriting expert. Without the Self-Proving Affidavit there is a bit more legal risk a Will won't be followed later. <u>But of people doing Wills about half skip a Self-Proving Affidavit</u> mostly due to the hassle of finding a notary on top of 2 witnesses each time a Will is done, and since it requires more work by the person doing a Will mostly just to save later work of people happy to be getting things under a Will.

FORM IS DONE BY TESTATOR AND 2 WITNESSES SIGNING WITH A NOTARY

For this form to be valid a person who is a notary (also called a "notary public") must see the Testator and 2 witnesses sign this form and then the notary notarizes the form. A notary can be found and asked to help at a bank, copy-mail center, brokers, insurance agents, library, court, government office, and many other places (using a phonebook to find a helpful notary is common). This form is often signed a few minutes after a Will is signed but it can be done later (even years later) when all can meet with a notary. But this Affidavit form <u>can't legally be done before</u> the Will it supports is done. This form when completed is often kept paper-clipped to the Will it supports.

SELF-PROVING AFFIDAVIT

STATE OF GEORGIA

COUNTY OF _____

    Before me, the undersigned authority, on this day personally appeared _____ (testator), _____ (witness), and _____ (witness), known to me to be the testator and the witnesses, respectively, whose names are subscribed to the annexed or foregoing instrument in their respective capacities, and all of said individuals being by me duly sworn, _____, testator, declared to me and to the witnesses in my presence that said instrument is the last will and testament and that the testator had willingly made and executed it as a free act and deed for the purposes expressed therein. The witnesses, each on oath, stated to me in the presence and hearing of the testator that the testator had declared to them that the instrument is the testator's last will and testament and that the testator executed the instrument as such and wished each of them to sign it as a witness; and under oath each witness stated further that the witness had signed the same as witness in the presence of the testator and at the testator's request; that the testator was 14 years of age or over and of sound mind; and that each of the witnesses was then at least 14 years of age.

_____
Testator

_____   _____
Witness   Witness

Sworn to and subscribed before me by _____, testator, and sworn to and subscribed before me by _____ and _____, witnesses, this __ day of _____, 20 __.

[NOTARY SEAL OR STAMP]   _____
                                                        Notary Public

CHAPTER 10
FORM 4: TANGIBLE PERSONAL PROPERTY GIFT LIST

FORM LETS GIFTS BE EASILY ADDED AFTER A WILL IS DONE

This form, often just called the "List" form, lets people after a Will is done easily write out more gifts of property to occur after death, but it is limited to covering "tangible personal property". This form is often also called a "Memorandum" or "Statement" or "Gift List". Georgia changed its law in 2021 to allow this form.

FORM GIVES EASY QUICK WAY TO WRITE GIFTS

The List form lets a person after a Will has been done write out more gifts of property to occur after death without the hassle of doing a new Will. <u>For a List form to be valid a Will must say they can be used</u>, and all this book's Wills say this. If a List form and a Will gift the same item then the Will is followed for that item. People can do many List form pages over time and all can count. If multiple List pages gift the same item the more recently done page controls for those items. People can slightly modify what a List form says by crossing out, erasing, or adding words, but then people should put a new date and signature at the bottom. People to cancel a List can rip it, mark it like with "X" or "void", or just throw it away so it is not found later. To reduce delays and uncertainty a List form not found within 90 days of the person's death will be ignored.

It may help understanding to <u>see the Georgia law about these List forms</u>, which says:

"Section 53-4-5 Written statement or list disposing of items of tangible personal property

(a) A written statement or list meeting the requirements of subsection (b) of this Code section shall dispose of items of tangible personal property, other than money, not otherwise specifically disposed of by the testator's will. If more than one otherwise effective writing exists, then, to the extent of any conflict among the writings, the provisions of a more recent writing revoke the inconsistent provisions of each prior writing.

(b) A written statement or list meets the requirements of this subsection if such writing:
  (1) Is signed and dated by the testator;
  (2) Describes the items and the beneficiaries with reasonable certainty; and
  (3) Is referred to in the testator's will.

The writing may be referred to as one to be in existence at the time of the testator's death; it may be prepared before or after the execution of the will; it may be altered by the testator after its preparation, provided that it is signed and dated on the date of such alteration; and it may be a writing that has no significance apart from its effect on the dispositions made by the will."

FORM CAN ONLY GIFT TANGIBLE PERSONAL PROPERTY

The List form can gift only "tangible personal property" so tangible (touchable) things (not accounts or most investments) and not "real property" (not land or buildings). It can't cover cash or coins even if old. Most lawyers recommend it not be used for business items. Improper property put in a form is ignored.

TO COMPLETE THE FORM SIGN AND DATE IT

To be valid a List form just must be signed and usually dated, and as said above a Will must say they are allowed. List form pages are often kept together and paper-clipped to a Will. People to cancel a List form can rip it up, mark it like with "X" or "void", or just throw it away so it is not found later.

TANGIBLE PERSONAL PROPERTY GIFT LIST

In this writing are gifts of tangible personal property to occur at my death including as provided by Georgia Code § 53-4-5. But this writing if not found by someone in the 90 days after my death is canceled and shall have no effect at all.

I may do many pages of these writings which should all be seen as one document. If there are conflicts among such writings the provisions of the more recent writing shall cancel the inconsistent provisions of a prior writing.

If a person getting a gift below does not survive me such gift is void and canceled.

DESCRIPTION OF PROPERTY	**NAME OF PERSONS TO GET PROPERTY**
_____ to	_____
_____ to	_____
_____ to	_____
_____ to	_____
_____ to	_____
_____ to	_____
_____ to	_____
_____ to	_____
_____ to	_____
_____ to	_____
_____ to	_____
_____ to	_____
_____ to	_____
_____ to	_____
_____ to	_____
_____ to	_____
_____ to	_____
_____ to	_____

DATE: _____ **SIGNED:** _____

CHAPTER 11
FORM 5: ADVANCE DIRECTIVE FOR HEALTH CARE

FORM CAN NAME HEALTH CARE AGENT AND GIVE INSTRUCTIONS

This form lets a person name someone to control health care if the person is later incapacitated and, also, give health care instructions. This chapter's form is copied exactly from a statutory form found in state law at Georgia Code § 31-32-4. Note, paramedics and similar people outside of a health facility are usually too busy to read and follow at all this long form, but if wanted people can do shorter forms (see next chapter).

CAN NAME "AGENT" TO HAVE POWER OVER HEALTH CARE IF NEEDED

The form lets a person name someone as "Health Care Agent" to control heath care if the person is later incapacitated. Note, a person controls their own health care by giving orders to doctors except when they are incapacitated by insufficient ability to a) communicate verbally or by notes, b) be rational, or c) be conscious. Often named to be Health Care Agent is a spouse, adult child, relative, or friend. Naming a family member as the Agent can avoid them having to rush to see judge to get power later in an emergency. A person's doctor or other person associated with a place giving them health care usually shouldn't be Agent unless they are closely related. A "Back-Up" Agent can be named but this is often skipped since it is rarely needed. In other states this kind of form is called a "Health Care Power Of Attorney" and the person getting power called the "Health Care Attorney-In-Fact".

IN FORM CAN GIVE TREATMENT PREFERENCES INCLUDING "LIVING WILL"

In the form a person can give written health care instructions that Agent, family, and doctors must follow. But many people skip writing instructions since they are hard to write to cover all situations, they can cause delay or lawsuits if not clear, and people trust their Agent's or family's wisdom maybe after talking to them. All people must do what a person wrote, and in other areas can use judgment to do what a person probably would want. People can name an Agent but skip instructions, or write instructions but not name an Agent. The "Treatment Preferences" part lets a person choose to say to stop health care if later the doctors find the person is in bad health and more care likely won't help, which choice many people call doing a "Living Will". Georgia unlike many states has no separate standard document for a Living Will since this 1 form covers it.

PERSON SIGNS FORM WITH 2 WITNESSES

To complete the form the person often signs while with 2 witnesses who also sign. Georgia law also lets a person "attest" the form (sign the form and later with a witness point at their signature and say it is theirs). Neither witness can be a person who is named Health Care Agent, likely to inherit or gain a financial benefit from the person's death, or is directly involved in the person's health care. Only 1 witness may work for any place providing health care. The form when completed usually should be quickly shown to any place that may give care to put in a person's medical file to follow. Usually a copy of the form also goes to the Agent. To cancel the form a person just says this to the Agent and maybe also tells any place that saw the form.

GEORGIA
ADVANCE DIRECTIVE FOR HEALTH CARE

By:_____
(Print Name)

Date of Birth:_____
(Month/Day/ Year)

This advance directive for health care has four parts:

PART ONE: HEALTH CARE AGENT. This part allows you to choose someone to make health care decisions for you when you cannot (or do not want to) make health care decisions for yourself. The person you choose is called a health care agent. You may also have your health care agent make decisions for you after your death with respect to an autopsy, organ donation, body donation, and final disposition of your body. You should talk to your health care agent about this important role.

PART TWO: TREATMENT PREFERENCES. This part allows you to state your treatment preferences if you have a terminal condition or if you are in a state of permanent unconsciousness. PART TWO will become effective only if you are unable to communicate your treatment preferences. Reasonable and appropriate efforts will be made to communicate with you about your treatment preferences before PART TWO becomes effective. You should talk to your family and others close to you about your treatment preferences.

PART THREE: GUARDIANSHIP. This part allows you to nominate a person to be your guardian should one ever be needed.

PART FOUR: EFFECTIVENESS AND SIGNATURES. This part requires your signature and the signatures of two witnesses. You must complete PART FOUR if you have filled out any other part of this form.

You may fill out any or all of the first three parts listed above. You must fill out PART FOUR of this form in order for this form to be effective.

You should give a copy of this completed form to people who might need it, such as your health care agent, your family, and your physician. Keep a copy of this completed form at home in a place where it can easily be found if it is needed. Review this completed form periodically to make sure it still reflects your preferences. If your preferences change, complete a new advance directive for health care.

Using this form of advance directive for health care is completely optional. Other forms of advance directives for health care may be used in Georgia.

You may revoke this completed form at any time. This completed form will replace any advance directive for health care, durable power of attorney for health care, health care proxy, or living will that you have completed before completing this form.

PART ONE: HEALTH CARE AGENT

[PART ONE will be effective even if PART TWO is not completed. A physician or health care provider who is directly involved in your health care may not serve as your health care agent. If you are married, a future divorce or annulment of your marriage will revoke the selection of your current spouse as your health care agent. If you are not married, a future marriage will revoke the selection of your health care agent unless the person you selected as your health care agent is your new spouse.]

(1) HEALTH CARE AGENT

I select the following person as my health care agent to make health care decisions for me:

Name:_____

Address:_____

Telephone Numbers:_____
                     (Home, Work, and Mobile)

(2) BACK-UP HEALTH CARE AGENT

***[This section is optional.** PART ONE will be effective even if this section is left blank.]*

If my health care agent cannot be contacted in a reasonable time period and cannot be located with reasonable efforts or for any reason my health care agent is unavailable or unable or unwilling to act as my health care agent, then I select the following, each to act successively in the order named, as my back-up health care agent(s):

Name:_____

Address:_____

Telephone Numbers:_____
                     (Home, Work, and Mobile)

Name:_____

Address:_____

Telephone Numbers:_____
                     (Home, Work, and Mobile)

(3) GENERAL POWERS OF HEALTH CARE AGENT

My health care agent will make health care decisions for me when I am unable to communicate my health care decisions or I choose to have my health care agent communicate my health care decisions.

My health care agent will have the same authority to make any health care decision that I could make. My health care agent's authority includes, for example, the power to:

- Admit me to or discharge me from any hospital, skilled nursing facility, hospice, or other health care facility or service;

- Request, consent to, withhold, or withdraw any type of health care; and

- Contract for any health care facility or service for me, and to obligate me to pay for these services (and my health care agent will not be financially liable for any services or care contracted for me or on my behalf).

My health care agent will be my personal representative for all purposes of federal or state law related to privacy of medical records (including the Health Insurance Portability and Accountability Act of 1996) to have the same access to my medical records that I have and can disclose the contents of my medical records to others for my ongoing health care.

My health care agent may accompany me in an ambulance or air ambulance if in the opinion of the ambulance personnel protocol permits a passenger, and my health care agent may visit or consult with me in person while I am in a hospital, skilled nursing facility, hospice, or other health care facility or service if its protocol permits visitation.

My health care agent may present a copy of this advance directive for health care in lieu of the original and the copy will have the same meaning and effect as the original.

I understand that under Georgia law:

- My health care agent may refuse to act as my health care agent;

- A court can take away the powers of my health care agent if it finds that my health care agent is not acting properly;

- My health care agent does not have the power to make health care decisions for me regarding sterilization, involuntary hospitalization, or involuntary treatment for mental or emotional illness, developmental disability, or addictive disease; and

- My health care agent does not have the power to make health care decisions that are otherwise covered under a psychiatric advance directive that I have executed pursuant to Chapter 11 of Title 37 of the Official Code of Georgia Annotated, including decisions related to treatment or hospitalization for mental or emotional illness, developmental disability, or addictive disease.

(4) GUIDANCE FOR HEALTH CARE AGENT

When making health care decisions for me, my health care agent should think about what action would be consistent with past conversations we have had, my treatment preferences as expressed in PART TWO (if I have filled out PART TWO), my religious and other beliefs and values, and how I have handled medical and other important issues in the past. If what I would decide is still unclear, then my health care agent should make decisions for me that my health care agent believes are in my best interest, considering the benefits, burdens, and risks of my current circumstances and treatment options.

(5) POWERS OF HEALTH CARE AGENT AFTER DEATH

(A) AUTOPSY

My health care agent will have the power to authorize an autopsy of my body unless I have limited my health care agent's power by initialing below.

_____ (Initials) My health care agent will not have the power to authorize an autopsy of my body (unless an autopsy is required by law).

(B) ORGAN DONATION AND DONATION OF BODY

My health care agent will have the power to make a disposition of any part or all of my body for medical purposes pursuant to the Georgia Revised Uniform Anatomical Gift Act, unless I have limited my health care agent's power by initialing below.

[Initial each statement that you want to apply.]

_____ (Initials) My health care agent will not have the power to make a disposition of my body for use in a medical study program.

_____ (Initials) My health care agent will not have the power to donate any of my organs.

(C) FINAL DISPOSITION OF BODY

My health care agent will have the power to make decisions about the final disposition of my body unless I have initialed below.

_____ (Initials) I want the following person to make decisions about the final disposition of my body:

Name:_____

Address:_____

Telephone Numbers:_____
                (Home, Work, and Mobile)

I wish for my body to be:

_____ (Initials) Buried

OR

_____ (Initials) Cremated

PART TWO: TREATMENT PREFERENCES

[PART TWO will be effective only if you are unable to communicate your treatment preferences after reasonable and appropriate efforts have been made to communicate with you about your treatment preferences. PART TWO will be effective even if PART ONE is not completed.
If you have not selected a health care agent in PART ONE, or if your health care agent is not available, then PART TWO will provide your physician and other health care providers with your treatment preferences. If you have selected a health care agent in PART ONE, then your health care agent will have the authority to make all health care decisions for you regarding matters covered by PART TWO. Your health care agent will be guided by your treatment preferences and other factors described in Section (4) of PART ONE.]

(6) CONDITIONS

PART TWO will be effective if I am in any of the following conditions:

[Initial each condition in which you want PART TWO to be effective.]

_____ (Initials) A terminal condition, which means I have an incurable or irreversible condition that will result in my death in a relatively short period of time.

_____ (Initials) A state of permanent unconsciousness, which means I am in an incurable or irreversible condition in which I am not aware of myself or my environment and I show no behavioral response to my environment.

My condition will be determined in writing after personal examination by my attending physician and a second physician in accordance with currently accepted medical standards.

(7) TREATMENT PREFERENCES

[State your treatment preference by initialing (A), (B), or (C). If you choose (C), state your additional treatment preferences by initialing one or more of the statements following (C). You may provide additional instructions about your treatment preferences in the next section. You will be provided with comfort care, including pain relief, but you may also want to state your specific preferences regarding pain relief in the next section.]

If I am in any condition that I initialed in Section (6) above and I can no longer communicate my treatment preferences after reasonable and appropriate efforts have been made to communicate with me about my treatment preferences, then:

(A) _____ (Initials) Try to extend my life for as long as possible, using all medications, machines, or other medical procedures that in reasonable medical judgment could keep me alive. If I am unable to take nutrition or fluids by mouth, then I want to receive nutrition or fluids by tube or other medical means.

OR

(B) _____ (Initials) Allow my natural death to occur. I do not want any medications, machines, or other medical procedures that in reasonable medical judgment could keep me alive but cannot cure me. I do not want to receive nutrition or fluids by tube or other medical means except as needed to provide pain medication.

OR

(C) _____ (Initials) I do not want any medications, machines, or other medical procedures that in reasonable medical judgment could keep me alive but cannot cure me, except as follows:

[Initial each statement that you want to apply to option (C).]

_____ (Initials) If I am unable to take nutrition by mouth, I want to receive nutrition by tube or other medical means.

_____ (Initials) If I am unable to take fluids by mouth, I want to receive fluids by tube or other medical means.

_____ (Initials) If I need assistance to breathe, I want to have a ventilator used.

_____ (Initials) If my heart or pulse has stopped, I want to have cardiopulmonary resuscitation (CPR) used.

(8) ADDITIONAL STATEMENTS

[This section is optional. PART TWO will be effective even if this section is left blank. This section allows you to state additional treatment preferences, to provide additional guidance to your health care agent (if you have selected a health care agent in PART ONE), or to provide information about your personal and religious values about your medical treatment. For example, you may want to state your treatment preferences regarding medications to fight infection, surgery, amputation, blood transfusion, or kidney dialysis. Understanding that you cannot foresee everything that could happen to you after you can no longer communicate your treatment preferences, you may want to provide guidance to your health care agent (if you have selected a health care agent in PART ONE) about following your treatment preferences. You may want to state your specific preferences regarding pain relief.]

(9) IN CASE OF PREGNANCY

[PART TWO will be effective even if this section is left blank.]

I understand that under Georgia law, PART TWO generally will have no force and effect if I am pregnant unless the fetus is not viable and I indicate by initialing below that I want PART TWO to be carried out.

_____ (Initials) I want PART TWO to be carried out if my fetus is not viable.

PART THREE: GUARDIANSHIP

(10) GUARDIANSHIP

[PART THREE is optional. This advance directive for health care will be effective even if PART THREE is left blank. If you wish to nominate a person to be your guardian in the event a court decides that a guardian should be appointed, complete PART THREE. A court will appoint a guardian for you if the court finds that you are not able to make significant responsible decisions for yourself regarding your personal support, safety, or welfare. A court will appoint the person nominated by you if the court finds that the appointment will serve your best interest and welfare. If you have selected a health care agent in PART ONE, you may (but are not required to) nominate the same person to be your guardian. If your health care agent and guardian are not the same person, your health care agent will have priority over your guardian in making your health care decisions, unless a court determines otherwise.]

[State your preference by initialing (A) or (B). Choose (A) only if you have also completed PART ONE.]

(A) _____ (Initials) I nominate the person serving as my health care agent under PART ONE to serve as my guardian.

OR

(B) _____ (Initials) I nominate the following person to serve as my guardian:

Name:_____

Address:_____

Telephone Numbers:_____
   (Home, Work, and Mobile)

PART FOUR: EFFECTIVENESS AND SIGNATURES

This advance directive for health care will become effective only if I am unable or choose not to make or communicate my own health care decisions.

This form revokes any advance directive for health care, durable power of attorney for health care, health care proxy, or living will that I have completed before this date.

Unless I have initialed below and have provided alternative future dates or events, this advance directive for health care will become effective at the time I sign it and will remain effective until my death (and after my death to the extent authorized in Section (5) of PART ONE).

_____ (Initials) This advance directive for health care will become effective on or upon _____ and will terminate on or upon _____ .

[You must sign and date or acknowledge signing and dating this form in the presence of two witnesses.

Both witnesses must be of sound mind and must be at least 18 years of age, but the witnesses do not have to be together or present with you when you sign this form.

A witness:

• Cannot be a person who was selected to be your health care agent or back-up health care agent in PART ONE;

• Cannot be a person who will knowingly inherit anything from you or otherwise knowingly gain a financial benefit from your death; or

• Cannot be a person who is directly involved in your health care.

Only one of the witnesses may be an employee, agent, or medical staff member of the hospital, skilled nursing facility, hospice, or other health care facility in which you are receiving health care (but this witness cannot be directly involved in your health care).]

SIGNATURE: By signing below, I state that I am emotionally and mentally capable of making this advance directive for health care and that I understand its purpose and effect.

_____   _____
(Signature of Declarant)   (Date)

WITNESSES:

The declarant signed this form in my presence or acknowledged signing this form to me. Based upon my personal observation, the declarant appeared to be emotionally and mentally capable of making this advance directive for health care and signed this form willingly and voluntarily.

_____   _____
(Signature of First Witness)   (Date)

Print Name:_____

Address:_____

_____   _____
(Signature of Second Witness)   (Date)

Print Name:_____

Address:_____

[This form does not need to be notarized.]

CHAPTER 12
FORM 6: DO NOT RESUSCITATE

FORMS DO SERIOUS ACT OF SAYING IMMEDIATELY DON'T GIVE MOST CARE

This chapter actually has 2 forms which are similar and do the serious act of saying to immediately no longer give most health care. Doing this is serious and usually only done by the very sickest or oldest people. Both forms are often called the "Do Not Resuscitate" or "DNR" form. This chapter's forms are copied exactly from the standard state forms. Both forms are short and usually will be followed by paramedics and other personnel outside any medical facility. Most facilities a person may be inside also will follow these forms.

FIRST FORM SAYS TO IMMEDIATELY NOT GIVE MANY KINDS OF CARE

This first form, the "Physician Orders For Life Sustaining Treatment" form (the "P.O.L.S.T." form) says to immediately not give most health care. In the form a person picks options and often says to immediately no longer give antibiotics, artificial feeding, or resuscitation (this includes cardio-pulmonary resuscitation (C.P.R.). This form is short so it can be read fast and followed by those in a hurry like paramedics, but this form also can be used by people in a health care facility. Even if the form is done a person can still later go get pain medication or other comfort care including by calling for an ambulance to take them there. A person is usually free to cancel this form by telling a doctor or paramedic to give care. The P.O.L.S.T. form has become the main form used to say to immediately not give care, and other forms are used less often.

SECOND FORM SAYS TO IMMEDIATELY NOT TRY RESUSCITATION

This chapter's second form, the "Do Not Resuscitate Order" form", says to immediately not give any resuscitation, which is trying to restart or help breathing or the heart. Resuscitation usually also covers cardio-pulmonary resuscitation (C.P.R.), defibrillation (electric shocks), and machine or tube breathing. This form is short so it can be read fast and followed by those in a hurry like paramedics, but this form also can be used by people in a health care facility. Even if this form has been done a person can still go, including by ambulance, to get pain medication and other comfort care. A person is usually free to override this form, like by telling a doctors or paramedics to now give all care. Some people wear a paper bracelet with Do Not Resuscitate Order information, or buy a metal bracelet from special Georgia companies.

FORM IS SIGNED BY DOCTOR AND PATIENT

A person's doctor usually has copies of the forms on special colored paper and will help fill these out. To be valid form either of these forms must be signed by a person's doctor or similar health professional, and by the person doing the form or their representative (like a person's Health Care Agent). Once the form is done people usually people show it to all places that may give care to add it to medical files to follow. Usually the person also keeps a copy of the form by their bed, on their refrigerator, or on or near their body to show to paramedics or others who may try to give care.

PHYSICIAN ORDERS FOR LIFE- SUSTAINING TREATMENT (POLST)

Patient's Name _____ _____ _____
(First) (Middle) (Last)
Date of Birth _____ **Gender:** Male ☐ Female ☐

A **CODE STATUS** Check One	**CARDIOPULMONARY RESUSCITATION (CPR): Patient has no pulse and is not breathing.** ☐ **Attempt Resuscitation (CPR).** ☐ **Allow Natural Death (AND) - Do Not Attempt Resuscitation.** ** *Signature of a concurring physician is needed for this section to be valid **if** this form is signed by an Authorized Person who is not the Health Care Agent. See additional guidance under III on back of form.* **When not in cardiopulmonary arrest, follow orders in B, C and D.**
B Check One	**MEDICAL INTERVENTIONS: Patient has pulse and /or is breathing.** ☐ **Comfort Measures**: Use medication by any route, positioning, wound care, and other measures to relieve pain and suffering. Use oxygen, suction, and manual treatment of airway obstruction as needed for comfort. *Do not transfer to hospital for life-sustaining treatment.* ☐ **Limited Additional Interventions**: In addition to treatment and care described above, provide medical treatment, as indicated. DO NOT USE intubation or mechanical ventilation. *Transfer to hospital if indicated. Generally avoid intensive care unit.* ☐ **Full Treatment**: In addition to treatment and care described above, use intubation, mechanical ventilation, and cardioversion as indicated. *Transfer to hospital and/or intensive care unit if indicated.* Additional Orders (e.g. dialysis):
C Check One	**ANTIBIOTICS** ☐ No antibiotics: Use other measures to relieve symptoms. ☐ Determine use or limitation of antibiotics when infection occurs. ☐ Use antibiotics if life can be prolonged. Additional Orders:
D Check One In Each Column	**ARTIFICIALLY ADMINISTERED NUTRITION/FLUIDS** **Where indicated, always offer food or fluids by mouth if feasible** ☐ No artificial nutrition by tube. ☐ No IV fluids. ☐ Trial period of artificial nutrition by tube. ☐ Trial period of IV fluids. ☐ Long-term artificial nutrition by tube. ☐ Long-term IV fluids. Additional Orders: Additional Orders:

DISCUSSION AND SIGNATURES
The basis for these orders should be documented in the medical record. To the best of my knowledge these orders are consistent with the patient's current medical condition and preferences and comply with the requirements of applicable Georgia law.

Physician Name:	Physician Signature:	Date:
License No.: State:		Phone:
Concurring Physician Name (*if needed; see III.i. on back of form*): License No.: State:	Concurring Physician Signature (if needed):	Date: Phone:
Patient or Authorized Person Name: ****authorized person may NOT sign if patient has decision making capacity*	Patient or Authorized Person Signature:	Date: Phone:

Relationship to Patient (check all that apply):
☐ Self ☐ Health Care Agent ☐ Spouse ☐ Court-Appointed Guardian ☐ Son or Daughter ☐ Parent ☐ Brother or Sister

GUIDANCE FOR COMPLETING THE POLST FORM

1. Completion of a POLST form is <u>always voluntary</u>.
2. Any section of a POLST form which is not completed implies full treatment for interventions discussed in that section.
3. A POLST form may be executed/created:
    a. when a patient has a serious illness or condition and the attending physician's reasoned judgment is that the patient will die within the next 365 days <u>OR</u>
    b. at any time if a person has been diagnosed with dementia or another progressive, degenerative disease or condition that attacks the brain and results in impaired memory, thinking, and behavior.
4. **If the patient has decision making capacity**, that patient chooses whether to complete and sign the POLST form with his or her physician. An authorized person may <u>NOT</u> sign the POLST form for a patient who has decision making capacity.
5. **If the patient lacks decision making capacity**, the POLST form may be signed by an "authorized person", which includes, in the following order of priority:
    a. the agent named on the patient's durable power of attorney for health care <u>or</u> a health care agent named on the patient's advance directive for health care
    b. a spouse
    c. a court-appointed guardian
    d. son or daughter (age 18 or older)
    e. parent
    f. brother or sister (age 18 or older)
6. If an authorized person completes and signs the POLST form, treatment choices should be based in good faith on what the patient would have wanted if the patient understood his or her current circumstances.

ADDITIONAL GUIDANCE FOR HEALTH CARE PROFESSIONALS

I. When a POLST form is signed by the <u>Patient</u> and Attending Physician, all orders may be implemented without restriction.
II. When a POLST form is signed by the patient's <u>Health Care Agent</u> and Attending Physician:
   i. If Section A indicates Allow Natural Death – Do Not Attempt Resuscitation, this order may be implemented when the patient is a "candidate for non-resuscitation"* as defined in Georgia Code Section 31-39-2(4). However, a concurring physician signature is <u>NOT</u> required per Georgia Code Section 31-92-4(c).
   ii. Orders in Sections B, C and D may be implemented without restriction.
III. When a POLST form is signed by an <u>Authorized Person</u> (other than the patient's Health Care Agent) and Attending Physician:
   i. If Section A indicates Allow Natural Death – Do Not Attempt Resuscitation, this order may be implemented when the patient is a "candidate for non-resuscitation"* as defined in Georgia Code Section 31-39-2(4). A concurring physician signature is <u>REQUIRED</u> per Georgia Code Section 31-39-4(c).
   ii. Orders in B, C, or D may be implemented when patient is:
      a. in a terminal condition <u>OR</u>
      b. state of permanent unconsciousness <u>OR</u>
      c. diagnosed with dementia or another progressive, degenerative disease or condition that attacks the brain and results in impaired memory, thinking and behavior.
IV. **The status of resuscitation orders during surgery or other invasive procedures should be reviewed** by the physician with the patient or patient's "authorized person" (as defined above).
V. Copies of the original POLST form are valid.
VI. The POLST form shall remain effective unless revoked by the attending physician upon the consent of the patient or the patient's authorized person.
VII. An attending physician who issues an order using the POLST form and who transfers the patient to another physician shall inform the receiving physician and the health care facility, if applicable, of the order.
VIII. A health care facility may impose additional administrative or procedural requirements regarding a patient's end of life care decisions, including the use of a separate order form. If the patient is in a health care facility, the attending physician should check with the facility to ensure these orders are valid.

* Georgia Code Section 31-92-2(4) defines a "candidate for non-resuscitation" to mean a patient who, based on a reasonable degree of medical certainty:
   (A) has a medical condition which can reasonably be expected to result in the imminent death of the patient;
   (B) is in a non-cognitive state with no reasonable possibility of regaining cognitive functions; or
   (C) is a person for whom CPR would be medically futile in that such resuscitation will likely be unsuccessful in restoring cardiac and respiratory function or will only restore cardiac and respiratory function for a brief period of time so that the patient will likely experience repeated need for CPR over a short period of time or that such resuscitation would be otherwise medically futile.

SUBSEQUENT REVIEW OF THE POLST FORM

This form should be reviewed when (i) the patient is transferred from one care setting or care level to another (ii) released to return home (iii) there is substantial change in the patient's health status, or (iv) the patient's treatment preferences change. If this POLST is voided, replaced, or becomes invalid, then draw a line through sections A though D, write "VOID" in large letters with date and time, and sign by the line. After voiding the form, a new form may be completed. *If no new form is completed, full treatment and resuscitation may be provided.*

Date/Time of Review	Location of Review	Print Name of Reviewer	Outcome of Review	Physician Signature
			☐ No Change ☐ Form Voided, new form completed ☐ Form Voided, no new form	
			☐ No Change ☐ Form Voided, new form completed ☐ Form Voided, no new form	

DO NOT RESUSCITATE ORDER

NAME OF PATIENT: _____

THIS CERTIFIES THAT AN ORDER NOT TO RESUSCITATE HAS BEEN ENTERED ON THE ABOVE-NAMED PATIENT.

                      SIGNED: _____
                                          ATTENDING PHYSICIAN

PRINTED OR TYPED NAME OF ATTENDING PHYSICIAN:

_____

ATTENDING PHYSICIAN'S TELEPHONE NUMBER: _____

DATE: _____

Bracelet / Necklace Optional

A person who is not in a hospital, nursing home or licensed hospice and has an order not to resuscitate **may** wear an identifying bracelet on either the wrist or the ankle or an identifying necklace and shall post or place a prominent notice in the person's home or residence to provide notice of the order not to resuscitate.

If such bracelet or necklace is worn, it shall be substantially similar to identification bracelets worn in hospitals and shall provide the following information in boldface type:

DO NOT RESUSCITATE ORDER

Patient's name: _____

Authorized person's name and telephone number, if applicable:
_____
_____

Patient's physician's printed name and telephone number:
_____

Date of order not to resuscitate: _____

CHAPTER 13
FORM 7: STATUTORY FORM POWER OF ATTORNEY

FORM LETS POWER BE GIVEN OVER PROPERTY, MONEY, AND MORE

The form lets a person give power to someone to do things with the person's money, property, debt, and more. Some people this a "Financial Power Of Attorney" or a "Standard Power Of Attorney". This chapter's form is <u>copied exactly from a statutory form</u> found in state law at Georgia Code § 10-6B-70.

FORM GIVES POWER TO LET SOMEONE HELP WITH PROPERTY AND MONEY

Form lets "Principal" give power to "Agent" or "Attorney-in-Fact" to do things involving Principal's money, property, and other things. Often Agent is a trusted person like spouse, relative, or friend. This form lets Agent help do chores, pay bills, move money in accounts, buy or sell items, sign contracts, take out debt, and get information from others. This can help if person is sick, busy, or away. The form may help person stay home and not need nursing home or a court doing something. People with capacity still have power and can overrule or fire an Agent. Naming "Successor Agents" is usually skipped since it is rarely needed. In form a person can say who should be "Conservator" if one is needed, and usually they name the Agent. Later if Agent signs things it should be like, "Ed Doe signing as Agent under Power of Attorney for Ann Po".

FORM LETS PERSON PICK POWERS TO GIVE

Form has place to initial to pick powers of Agent but to avoid possible problems usually people give much power, like by initialing line saying "All Preceding Powers". In "Grant of Specific Authority" area are extra dangerous powers (like power to gift away money and property) and many people don't give these.

DUE TO RISKS INCLUDING FRAUD MANY SKIP FORM OR CONSULT A LAWYER

Using this form can be risky and lead to loss of money and property since an Agent can do dumb or criminal actions like stealing property, wasting money on dumb items, or just causing harm by carelessness. Agents have a "duty of care" and can be sued later but they might be out of money so can't undo their harm. Usually banks or others can't be blamed for obeying an Agent. Many people ask a lawyer for advice.

IT MAY BE IMPROPER FOR AGENT TO MAKE GIFTS OR DO OTHER THINGS

This area of law is complex and basic acts may be fine like paying bills, moving funds, or getting records. But less usual acts may be improper and even a crime by Agent like as gift handing out money or property to family or friends, making risky investments, or doing unusual acts. Many people ask a lawyer for advice.

PERSON SIGNS FORM WITH A NOTARY AND 1 WITNESS

The form should be signed by the person doing it in front of a notary and 1 witness, and then the witness signs the form and the notary notarizes the form. The person who is witness can't be named as Agent in the form. Once signed the form can be kept till needed or given quickly to Agent to hold and use. To cancel the form a person should tell the Agent and take back copies, and maybe tell people that saw it. <u>The last page is a totally separate and optional page</u> that a bank may later (often years later) request be done, and the Agent can sign it while with a person who is a notary who then notarizes the form.

State of Georgia

County of _____

GEORGIA
STATUTORY FORM POWER OF ATTORNEY

IMPORTANT INFORMATION

This power of attorney authorizes another person (your agent) to make decisions concerning your property for you (the principal). Your agent will be able to make decisions and act with respect to your property (including your money) whether or not you are able to act for yourself. The meaning of authority over subjects listed on this form is explained in O.C.G.A. Chapter 6B of Title 10.

This power of attorney does not authorize the agent to make health care decisions for you.

You should select someone you trust to serve as your agent. Unless you specify otherwise in the Special Instructions, generally the agent's authority will continue until you die or revoke the power of attorney or the agent resigns or is unable to act for you.

Your agent is not entitled to any compensation unless you state otherwise in the Special Instructions. Your agent shall be entitled to reimbursement of reasonable expenses incurred in performing the acts required by you in your power of attorney.

This form provides for designation of one agent. If you wish to name more than one agent, you may name a successor agent or name a coagent in the Special Instructions. Coagents will not be required to act together unless you include that requirement in the Special Instructions.

If your agent is unable or unwilling to act for you, your power of attorney will end unless you have named a successor agent. You may also name a second successor agent.

This power of attorney shall be durable unless you state otherwise in the Special Instructions.

This power of attorney becomes effective immediately unless you state otherwise in the Special Instructions.

If you have questions about the power of attorney or the authority you are granting to your agent, you should seek legal advice before signing this form.

DESIGNATION OF AGENT

I _____ (Name of principal)
name the following person as my agent:

Name of agent: _____
Address: _____
Phone: _____ Email: _____

DESIGNATION OF SUCCESSOR AGENT(S) (OPTIONAL)

If my agent is unable or unwilling to act for me, I name as my successor agent:

Name of successor agent: _____
Address: _____
Phone: _____ Email: _____

If my successor agent is unable or unwilling to act for me, I name as my second successor agent:

Name of second successor agent: _____
Address: _____
Phone: _____ Email: _____

GRANT OF GENERAL AUTHORITY

I grant my agent and any successor agent general authority to act for me with respect to the following subjects as defined in O.C.G.A. Chapter 6B of Title 10:

(INITIAL each subject you want to include in the agent's general authority. If you wish to grant general authority over all of the subjects, you may initial all preceding subjects instead of initialing each subject.)

(_____) Real property
(_____) Tangible personal property
(_____) Stocks and bonds
(_____) Commodities and options
(_____) Banks and other financial institutions
(_____) Operation of entity or business
(_____) Insurance and annuities
(_____) Estates, trusts, and other beneficial interests
(_____) Claims and litigation
(_____) Personal and family maintenance
(_____) Benefits from governmental programs or civil or military service
(_____) Retirement plans
(_____) Taxes
(_____) **All preceding subjects**

GRANT OF SPECIFIC AUTHORITY (OPTIONAL)

My agent SHALL NOT do any of the following specific acts for me UNLESS I have INITIALED the specific authority listed below:

(CAUTION: Granting any of the following will give your agent the authority to take actions that could significantly reduce your property or change how your property is distributed at your death. INITIAL ONLY the specific authority you WANT to give your agent. You should give your agent specific instructions in the Special Instructions when you authorize your agent to make gifts.)

(_____) Create, fund, amend, revoke, or terminate an inter vivos trust

(_____) Make a gift, subject to the limitations of O.C.G.A. 10-6B-56 and any Special Instructions in this power of attorney

(_____) Create or change rights of survivorship

(_____) Create or change a beneficiary designation

(_____) Authorize another person to exercise the authority granted under this power of Attorney

(_____) Waive the principal's right to be a beneficiary of a joint and survivor annuity, including a survivor benefit under a retirement plan

(_____) Exercise authority over the content of electronic communications sent or received by the principal

(_____) Exercise fiduciary powers that the principal has authority to delegate and that are expressly and clearly identified (including the persons for which the principal acts as a fiduciary) in the Special Instructions

(_____) Renounce an interest in property, including a power of appointment

LIMITATION ON AGENT'S AUTHORITY

An agent that is not my ancestor, spouse, or descendant SHALL NOT use my property to benefit the agent or a person to whom the agent owes an obligation of support unless I have included that authority in the Special Instructions.

SPECIAL INSTRUCTIONS (OPTIONAL)

You may give special instructions on the following lines (you may add lines or place your special instructions in a separate document and attach it to the power of attorney):

EFFECTIVE DATE

This power of attorney is effective immediately unless I have stated otherwise in the Special Instructions.

NOMINATION OF CONSERVATOR (OPTIONAL)

If it becomes necessary for a court to appoint a conservator of my estate, I nominate the following person(s) for appointment:

Name of nominee for conservator of my estate:_____
Address: _____
Phone:_____ Email:_____

RELIANCE ON THIS POWER OF ATTORNEY

Any person, including my agent, may rely upon the validity of this power of attorney or a copy of it unless that person has actual knowledge it has terminated or is invalid.

SIGNATURE AND ACKNOWLEDGMENT

Your signature:_____ Date:_____

Your name printed:_____
Your address:_____
Your phone:_____ Your email:_____

(WITNESS)

This document was signed or acknowledged in my presence on
_____ by _____.
(Date)   (Name of Principal)

Witness signature:_____ Date:_____

Witness name printed:_____
Witness address:_____
Witness phone:_____ Witness email:_____

(NOTARY)

State of Georgia

County of _____

This document was signed or acknowledged in my presence on
_____ by _____.
(Date)   (Name of Principal)

(Seal)   Signature of notary:_____
                      Commission expires:_____

IMPORTANT INFORMATION FOR AGENT

Agent's Duties

When you accept the authority granted under this power of attorney, a special legal relationship is created between you and the principal. This relationship imposes upon you legal duties that continue until you resign or the power of attorney is terminated or revoked. You must:

(1) Do what you know the principal reasonably expects you to do with the principal's property or, if you do not know the principal's expectations, act in the principal's best interest;

(2) Act in good faith;

(3) Do nothing beyond the authority granted in this power of attorney; and

(4) Disclose your identity as an agent whenever you act for the principal by writing or printing the name of the principal and signing your own name as agent in the following manner: (Principal's name) by (Your signature) as Agent.

Unless the Special Instructions in this power of attorney state otherwise, you must also:

(1) Act loyally for the principal's benefit;

(2) Avoid conflicts that would impair your ability to act in principal's best interest;

(3) Act with care, competence, and diligence;

(4) Keep a record of all receipts, disbursements, and transactions made on behalf of the principal;

(5) Cooperate with any person that has authority to make health care decisions for the principal to do what you know the principal reasonably expects or, if you do not know the principal's expectations, to act in the principal's best interest; and

(6) Attempt to preserve the principal's estate plan if you know the plan and preserving the plan is consistent with the principal's best interest.

Termination of Agent's Authority

You must stop acting on behalf of the principal if you learn of any event that terminates this power of attorney or your authority under this power of attorney. Events that terminate a power of attorney or your authority to act under a power of attorney include:

(1) Death of the principal;

(2) The principal's revocation of your authority or the power of attorney;

(3) The occurrence of a termination event stated in the power of attorney;

(4) The purpose of the power of attorney is fully accomplished; or

(5) If you are married to the principal, a legal action is filed with a court to end your marriage, or for your legal separation, unless the Special Instructions in this power of attorney state that such an action will not terminate your authority.

Liability of Agent

The meaning of the authority granted to you is defined in O.C.G.A. Chapter 6B of Title 10. If you violate O.C.G.A. Chapter 6B of Title 10 or act outside the authority granted, you may be liable for any damages caused by your violation.

If there is anything about this document or your duties that you do not understand, you should seek legal advice.

AGENT'S CERTIFICATION AS TO THE VALIDITY OF POWER OF ATTORNEY AND AGENT'S AUTHORITY

(Georgia Code § 10-6B-71; This form may be used later by an agent to support a power of attorney.)

State of Georgia

County of _____

I, _____ (name of agent), certify under penalty of perjury that _____ (name of principal) granted me authority as an agent or successor agent in a power of attorney dated _____.

I further certify that to my knowledge:

(1) The principal is alive and has not revoked the power of attorney or my authority to act under the power of attorney and the power of attorney and my authority to act under the power of attorney have not terminated;
(2) If the power of attorney was drafted to become effective upon the happening of an event or contingency, the event or contingency has occurred;
(3) If I were named as a successor agent, the prior agent is no longer able or willing to serve; and
(4) _____
_____
_____.

(Insert other relevant statements)

SIGNATURE AND ACKNOWLEDGMENT

_____   _____
Agent's signature   Date

_____   _____
Agent's name printed   Agent's telephone number

_____
Agent's address

_____
Agent's email address

NOTARY: This document was signed in my presence on _____ (Date), by _____ (Name of agent).

(Seal)

_____
Signature of notary
My commission expires:_____

CHAPTER 14
FORM 8: POWER OF ATTORNEY TO DELEGATE THE POWER AND AUTHORITY FOR THE CARE OF A CHILD

FORM LETS PARENT GIVE POWER TO SOMEONE OVER MINOR CHILD

This form lets a parent give power over a minor child under age 18 to person they name. This chapter's form is copied from the statutory form found in state law at Georgia Code § 19-9-134. This form is also available online on the internet webpages of some courts, schools, and agencies in Georgia, like at https://gwinnettflc.atlantalegalaid.org/wp-content/uploads/2018/09/Power-of-Attorney-of-Minor-Child.pdf .

FORM CAN DESIGNATE SOMEONE TO HAVE POWER OVER CHILD

In the form a parent can name someone as "Agent" to have power over a minor child under age 18. A person to be Agent must be at least 18 and a Georgia resident. Georgia law since 2021 no longer limits giving power to just grandparents, but schools, doctors, and other people feel more comfortable and willing to follow the form if a grandparent gets power (so picking a child's grandparent is strongly recommended). This form is technically a "power of attorney" kind of form so the Agent is also called the "attorney-in-fact". This form can let a friend, relative, teacher, or other person if needed make decisions about child's health care, school, food, home, or discipline. This form is often used if a parent is away from child for work, prison or jail, school, sports, drug treatment, immigration, military, weeks long visit with family or friends, or if a child is sick in hospital and needs someone with power close by. A parent keeps power so really power is shared, and the parent can fire the Agent or overrule a decision. Note, this form is not usually done for brief things like a couple day visit with family, weekend sleep-over with friends, or a few hours or days with a babysitter.

FORM COVERS POWERS GIVEN, TIME DURATION, AND BACKGROUND CHECKS

In the form a person can say either a) all powers a parent has are given (which is common to avoid legal issues) or b) limited powers handwritten into form are given (this is rarely used). In the form the duration can be chosen and a) most people pick 1 year the maximum, b) if power goes to grandparent there is no time limit, and c) military people can set it to length of deployment. As the form says if the Agent isn't related to a child a background check is often required. Picking a child's grandparent is strongly recommended

PERSON SIGNS WITH NOTARY AND LATER AGENT SIGNS THE ACCEPTANCE

Both 2 parents must sign the form in front of a notary if both are alive and both have joint legal custody, otherwise 1 parent signing is sufficient. The law at Georgia Code § 19-9-125 (which people can look up) explains a parent without legal custody needn't sign but should get certified mail notice without 15 days after which they have 21 days to object for good reason (this is rare). The last page (called "Acceptance") can be done later (often months later) when the person who got power is trying to use the form, and they should sign this page while with a person who is notary who then notarizes the form. To cancel the form before it is set to end a parent should tell the person who got power it is canceled and take back copies, and also maybe tell places that saw the form that it is canceled.

FORM FOR
POWER OF ATTORNEY TO DELEGATE
THE POWER AND AUTHORITY FOR THE CARE OF A CHILD

NOTICE:

(1) THE PURPOSE OF THIS POWER OF ATTORNEY IS TO GIVE THE INDIVIDUAL WHOM YOU DESIGNATE (THE AGENT) POWERS TO CARE FOR YOUR CHILD, INCLUDING THE POWER TO: HAVE ACCESS TO EDUCATIONAL RECORDS AND DISCLOSE THE CONTENTS TO OTHERS; ARRANGE FOR AND CONSENT TO MEDICAL, DENTAL, AND MENTAL HEALTH TREATMENT FOR THE CHILD; HAVE ACCESS TO RECORDS RELATED TO SUCH TREATMENT OF THE CHILD AND DISCLOSE THE CONTENTS OF THOSE RECORDS TO OTHERS; PROVIDE FOR THE CHILD'S FOOD, LODGING, RECREATION, AND TRAVEL; AND HAVE ANY ADDITIONAL POWERS AS SPECIFIED BY THE INDIVIDUAL EXECUTING THIS POWER OF ATTORNEY.

(2) THE AGENT IS REQUIRED TO EXERCISE DUE CARE TO ACT IN THE CHILD'S BEST INTERESTS AND IN ACCORDANCE WITH THE GRANT OF AUTHORITY SPECIFIED IN THIS FORM.

(3) A COURT OF COMPETENT JURISDICTION MAY REVOKE THE POWERS OF THE AGENT.

(4) THE AGENT MAY EXERCISE THE POWERS GIVEN IN THIS POWER OF ATTORNEY FOR THE CARE OF A CHILD FOR THE PERIOD SET FORTH IN THIS FORM UNLESS THE INDIVIDUAL EXECUTING THIS POWER OF ATTORNEY REVOKES THIS POWER OF ATTORNEY AND PROVIDES NOTICE OF THE REVOCATION TO THE AGENT OR A COURT OF COMPETENT JURISDICTION TERMINATES THIS POWER OF ATTORNEY.

(5) THE AGENT MAY RESIGN AS AGENT AND MUST IMMEDIATELY COMMUNICATE SUCH RESIGNATION TO THE INDIVIDUAL EXECUTING THIS POWER OF ATTORNEY AND TO SCHOOLS, HEALTH CARE PROVIDERS, AND OTHERS KNOWN TO THE AGENT TO HAVE RELIED UPON SUCH POWER OF ATTORNEY.

(6) THIS POWER OF ATTORNEY MAY BE REVOKED IN WRITING. IF THIS POWER OF ATTORNEY IS REVOKED, THE REVOKING INDIVIDUAL SHALL NOTIFY THE AGENT, SCHOOLS, HEALTH CARE PROVIDERS, AND OTHERS KNOWN TO THE INDIVIDUAL EXECUTING THIS POWER OF ATTORNEY TO HAVE RELIED UPON SUCH POWER OF ATTORNEY.

(7) IF THERE IS ANYTHING ABOUT THIS FORM THAT YOU DO NOT UNDERSTAND, YOU SHOULD ASK AN ATTORNEY TO EXPLAIN IT TO YOU.

STATE OF GEORGIA
COUNTY OF _____

Personally appeared before me, the undersigned officer duly authorized to administer oaths, _____ (name of parent) who, after having been sworn, deposes and says as follows:

1. I certify that I am the parent of:

_____
    (Full name of child)   (Date of birth)

2. I designate: _____ ,
                            (Full name of agent)

_____
    (Street address, city, state, and ZIP Code of agent)

_____ ,
    (Personal and work telephone numbers of agent)

as the agent of the child named above.

3. The agent named above is related or known to me as follows *(write in your relationship to the agent; for example, aunt of the child, maternal grandparent of the child, sibling of the child, god-parent of the child, associated with a nonprofit or faith based organization)*:

_____

4. Sign by the statement you wish to choose (you may only choose one):

(A) _____ (Signature) The agent named above is related to me by blood or marriage and I have elected not to have him or her obtain a criminal background check.

OR

(B) _____ (Signature) The agent named above is not related to me and I have reviewed his or her criminal background check. *(If the agent has a criminal conviction, complete the rest of this paragraph.)* I know that the agent has a conviction but I want him or her to be the agent because *(write in)*:

_____

_____

5. Sign by the statement you wish to choose *(you may only choose one)*:

(A) _____ (Signature) I delegate to the agent **all my power and authority regarding the care and custody of the child named above**, including but not limited to the right to inspect and obtain copies of educational records and other records concerning the child, attend school activities and other functions concerning the child, and give or withhold any consent or waiver with respect to school activities, medical and dental treatment, and any other activity, function, or treatment that may concern the child. This delegation shall not include the power or authority to consent to the marriage or adoption of the child, the performance or inducement of an abortion on or for the child, or the termination of parental rights to the child.

OR

(B) _____ (Signature) I delegate to the agent the following specific powers and responsibilities *(write in):*

_____
_____
_____
_____
_____
_____
_____
_____
_____
_____
_____
_____

This delegation shall not include the power or authority to consent to the marriage or adoption of the child, the performance or inducement of an abortion on or for the child, or the termination of parental rights to the child.

6. Initial by the statement you wish to choose *(you may only choose one of the three options)* and complete the information in the paragraph:

(A) _____ (Initials) This power of attorney is effective for a period not to exceed one year, beginning _____, 20____, and ending _____, 20____. I reserve the right to revoke this power and authority at any time.

OR

(B) _____ (Initials) This power of attorney is being given to a grandparent of my child and is effective until I revoke this power of attorney.

OR

(C) _____ (Initials) I am a parent as described in O.C.G.A. § 19-9-132(b). My deployment is scheduled to begin on , 2, and is estimated to end on , 2. I acknowledge that in no event shall this delegation of power and authority last more than one year or the term of my deployment plus 30 days, whichever is longer. I reserve the right to revoke this power and authority at any time.

7. I hereby swear or affirm under penalty of law that I provided the notice required by O.C.G.A. § 19-9-125 and received no objection in the required time period.

By: _____   _____
(Parent signature)   (Printed name)

_____
(Street address, city, state, and ZIP Code of parent)

_____
(Personal and work telephone numbers of parent)

Sworn to and subscribed before me this
_____day of _____, 20_____.

_____
Notary public   (SEAL)
My commission expires:_____

STATE OF GEORGIA
COUNTY OF _____

ACCEPTANCE BY AGENT

Personally appeared before me, the undersigned officer duly authorized to administer oaths, _____ (name of agent) who, after having been sworn, deposes and says as follows:

8. I hereby accept my designation as agent for the child specified in this power of attorney and by doing so acknowledge my acceptance of the responsibility for caring for such child for the duration of this power of attorney. Furthermore, I hereby certify that:

(A)(i) I am related to the individual giving me this power of attorney by blood or marriage as follows *(write in your relationship to the individual designating you as agent; for example, sister, mother, father, etc.)*: _____
OR
(ii) I am not related to the individual giving me this power of attorney but was referred to him or her by: _____ *(write in the name of the child-placing agency, nonprofit entity, or faith based organization)*.

(B) I am not currently on the state sexual offender registry of this state or the sexual offender registry or child abuse registry for any other state, a United States territory, the District of Columbia, or any American Indian tribe nor have I ever been required to register for any such registry;

(C) I have provided a criminal background check to the individual designating me as an agent, if it was required;

(D) I understand that I have the authority to act on behalf of the child:
- For the period of time set forth in this form;
- Until the power of attorney is revoked in writing and notice is provided to me as required by O.C.G.A. § 19-9-130; or
- Until the power of attorney is terminated by order of a court;

(E) I understand that if I am made aware of the death of the individual who executed the power of attorney, I must notify the surviving parent of the child, if known, as soon as practicable; and

(F) I understand that I may resign as agent by notifying the individual who executed the power of attorney in writing by certified mail, return receipt requested, or statutory overnight delivery and I must also notify any schools, health care providers, and others to whom I give a copy of this power of attorney.

_____   _____
(Agent signature)   (Printed name)

Sworn to and subscribed before me this
_____ day of _____, 20____.
                                                                      (SEAL)

_____
Notary public
My commission expires: _____

_____   _____
(Organization signature, if applicable)   (Printed name and title)

CHAPTER 15
FORM 9: DESIGNATION TO CONTROL REMAINS

LETS PERSON BE NAMED TO CONTROL FUNERAL AND RELATED MATTERS

This form lets a person be named to control funeral and related matters. This chapter's form is <u>copied from a form</u> found in law at Georgia Code § 31-21-7. Note, the Advance Directive For Health Care form has a spot about if the Agent named there controls these issues so people can use that form instead of this form.

IN FORM CAN NAME AGENT TO CONTROL FUNERAL AND RELATED MATTERS

The form lets person <u>name someone to control their bodily remains</u> including related things like funeral, burial, cremation, ceremonies, religious services, dinners, tombstone, and buying goods or services for this. If this form is not done control of these things is by closest family (in order - a spouse, adult child, parent, and brothers or sisters). But people usually do this form only if family will be too upset, be bad with money, or do unwanted things. Payment for funeral and related matters comes from pre-paid funeral accounts, insurance, and the dead person's money and property, and Executor and family legally must help arrange payment. As already said in this book the Advance Directive For Health Care form has a spot to say if the Agent named there can control these issues, so people can use that instead of this chapter's form.

IN FORM INSTRUCTIONS CAN BE GIVEN WHICH EVERYONE SHOULD FOLLOW

The form has a spot to write some instructions but many people skip this and just trust the person given power to be wise or do what was discussed with them. Some people write instructions just to urge low cost. Importantly, if "Direct Burial" or "Direct Cremation" is requested the costs may be lower but this skips events involving the body till the time after a completed burial or cremation (so these occur without family watching). People including family should do funeral, burial, and related things a person wanted if the money and property in the decedent's estate can afford it.

SIGN FORM WITH NOTARY

The form must be signed by a person in front of a person who is a notary, and then the notary notarizes the form. The person doing this form is called the "Affiant". People should keep form in place it can be found within just 1 or 2 days of a death. It may help to tell famiy and friends where to find this form, or some people give the form to someone to hold. The form can be canceled by ripping it up, throwing it away, or clearly saying so, and then maybe tell all persons who have been shown the form that it is canceled.

DESIGNATION TO CONTROL REMAINS
Georgia Code § 31-21-7

State of Georgia

County of _____

I, _____, do hereby designate _____ with the right to control the disposition of my remains upon my death.

I (circle one) <u>have</u> <u>not</u> attached or written below specific directions concerning the disposition of my remains with which the designee shall substantially comply, provided such directions are lawful and there are sufficient resources in my estate to carry out the directions.

(Optional) DIRECTIONS: _____
_____
_____
_____
_____
_____
_____
_____

Signature of Affiant: _____

Subscribed and sworn to before me this ____ day of _____, 20___.

Signature of Notary Public: _____

APPENDIX:
SAMPLE FILLED OUT LEGAL FORMS

TO GET FORMS TO USE PEOPLE CAN:
   (1) PHOTOCOPY BOOK PAGES,
   (2) TEAR OUT PAGES FROM A BOOK, OR
   (3) DOWNLOAD BOOK WITH FORMS FROM WWW.DAVENPORTPUBLISHING.COM,
   AND USUALLY USING PDF FORM IS BEST TO AVOID SPACING/FORMAT CHANGES.

EMAIL ANY COMMENTS TO DAVENPORTPRESS@GMAIL.COM.

On the next pages to show how it can be done are some sample filled out legal forms.

People can add words to legal forms by computer or typewriter to be neater, but many people just by hand use pen, marker, or pencil to handwrite words into forms.

It is not required but better if signatures and dates are in ink or marker (not pencil).

Many parts of the forms especially spaces for Will gifts can be left empty and unfilled.

Anyone can fill in the words in a legal form not just the person doing the form, like a friend with neat writing can fill in all the words, addresses, and dates that are needed. Only the signatures must be done by each person doing the form for themselves.

When adding words in a form any of these is a fine way to do this:
        "I appoint ___*John Doe*___ as Agent",
        "I appoint ___John Doe___ as Agent",
        "I appoint John Doe as Agent".

When doing forms it may help to know "respectively" means "in the order just stated".

People need not worry about neatness or small mistakes, and a document is usually fine if those people who knew person during their life can tell the likely meaning.

Sample Filled Out Form: Will (Standard)
with Gifts section skipped to not bother making small gifts

LAST WILL AND TESTAMENT

I, __Paul Samuel Maxwell__, of __Gwinnett County__, Georgia, do revoke all prior Wills and testamentary documents and do make, publish, and declare this as my Will. I am of sound mind and under no duress or undue influence and act voluntarily.

1. LIVING SPOUSE AND CHILDREN. To show I am mentally fit and have sufficient memory to do a Will I do say I now have the following living spouse and living children:

_____none_____
_____.

2. GIFTS. I give these gifts in this Will, but to get a gift in this section the recipient must survive me except as otherwise stated below.

I give _____ to _____.
I give _____ to _____.
I give _____ to _____.
I give _____ to _____.
I give _____ to _____.
I give _____ to _____.

SKIPPED

3. SEPARATE WRITINGS. I may do writings separate from this Will to gift tangible personal property as allowed by state law, and all such writings should be followed. But any such writing not found within 90 days of my death is canceled and has no effect. A gift in such a writing to a person who does not survive me is canceled and has no effect. This Will does not revoke any such writings that now exist.

4. RESIDUE. The rest, residue, and remainder of my estate, and anything else, I give:

a) to __Susan Maxwell__ who survive me and with persons just named who survive me taking the share of non-survivors, then if anything remains

b) to __Oscar Adam Maxwell and Mary Ann Tabor__ and if any of those just now named do not survive me their part goes to their lineal descendants per stirpes.

62

5. ADMINISTRATION. I name, nominate, and appoint *Susan Maxwell my sister* as Personal Representative including for me, my Will, and my estate.

6. MISCELLANEOUS. The following applies to this Will and generally.

In this Will no part left unfilled is a mistake including spaces in the residue clause.

The facts support and I want Georgia state law to apply to this Will and my estate.

I order that my just debts, funeral and related expenses, and taxes be paid as soon after my death as practical but only those items my Personal Representative chooses to pay.

Any gift of money in this Will has priority over gifts in any separate writing.

Priority of Will gifts of the same type is based on the order they are made in this Will.

The words give and gift also means a devise, bequest, grant, legacy, or similar.

I am intentionally not providing by Will or other ways for some family, including I am not providing for some children of mine and also children of a deceased child of mine.

If a Will gift reasonably mentions survival then survival is an absolute condition and anti-lapse laws or similar provisions have no effect and without survival the gift lapses. Unless a Will gift specifies otherwise if a Will gift goes to multiple recipients if any do not survive me the part to them lapses and instead goes to other surviving recipients.

No earlier transfer reduces a Will gift unless I usually called it a loan or advancement.

In this Will any gendered word includes all genders, and the singular includes the plural and vice versa, and the word "they" can mean a single person or many persons.

Unless a Will specifically says otherwise a secured debt including a mortgage or lien shall not be paid off including by a Personal Representative or in probate, and a recipient of a Will gift of property takes it subject to debts. Also, no recipient of property who may lose it or who pays to keep it may have my estate or other people pay or do exoneration.

If I lost or no longer have an item in a Will specific gift then the gift is extinguished.

I request and authorize any informal, summary, and quick probate or similar action. Any Personal Representative may act independently with no supervision of any court, including independent administration, and with no inventory, appraisal, or other action.

I give any Personal Representative power to lease, sell, mortgage, convey, or keep property including real property in a manner and time they deem helpful or proper. I give any Personal Representative authority to settle or pay claims or debts in the time and manner they choose. I give any Personal Representative all powers and authority that may be given by statute or common law in any jurisdiction, including powers and authorities conferred by the Georgia Revised Probate Code of 1998 and Revised Georgia Trust Code of 2010, as amended, plus Georgia Code §§ 53-12-261 and 263 et seq., as amended.

Any Guardian of any type, Conservator, Custodian, or other person managing a minor's property or money may use or invade the principal and sell property without court action.

If context permits the terms Personal Representative and Executor and Administrator are interchangeable, Conservator and Guardian of the Estate and Guardian of Property and Custodian are interchangeable, and residue and residuary are interchangeable. Any such person may stand in the place of and have all powers like the others named here.

The residue includes lapsed or failed gifts, insurance paid to the estate, digital assets, inheritances owed me, and all I had power of appointment or testamentary disposition over.

Any Personal Representative may access, manage, delete, modify, transfer, and otherwise control any digital accounts and assets I had any interest in or power over.

Any Personal Representative, Executor, Administrator, Guardian of any type like for a person or estate, Conservator, Custodian, and any other fiduciary under this Will or otherwise shall qualify and serve without bond, surety, security, surety bond, or similar.

If evidence does not show it likely a person survived me by 120 hours (5 days) then for this Will and my estate they shall be deemed in all ways as having died before me.

Any Personal Representative may at any time transfer money or property of a minor under age 18 to a Custodian to act under the Georgia Uniform Transfers to Minors Act or similar law anywhere, and may pick a person to be Custodian including themselves.

If part of this Will is invalid or unenforceable other provisions shall remain in effect.

TESTATOR

IN WITNESS WHEREOF and in the presence of two witnesses, who are acting as witnesses at my request, in my presence and in the presence of each other, I hereunto sign my name on the _8th_ day of _January_, 20_23_.

Paul Samuel Maxwell
Signature of Testator

WITNESSES

The foregoing instrument was signed by the Testator in our presence and declared by the Testator to be the Testator's Will, and we, the undersigned witnesses, sign our names hereunto as witnesses at the request and in the presence of the Testator, and in the presence of each other on the _8th_ day of _January_, 20_23_.

Susan Ann Moon   14 2nd Street, Macon, GA 30318
Signature of Witness   Address of Witness

Eve Mable Smith   35 Buffalo Road, Denver, Colorado 80101
Signature of Witness   Address of Witness

Sample Filled Out Form: Will (Guardian)
with many gifts written in Gifts section, Guardian Clause used, and Residue Clause using percentages

LAST WILL AND TESTAMENT

I, __Paul Brian Baker__ of __Chatham County__, Georgia, do revoke all prior Wills and testamentary documents and do make, publish, and declare this as my Will. I am of sound mind and under no duress or undue influence and act voluntarily.

1. LIVING SPOUSE AND CHILDREN. To show I am mentally fit and have sufficient memory to do a Will I do say I now have the following living spouse and living children:

            __Ruth May Baker wife__   __Oscar Elliot Baker young son__
            __Karen Lisa Lundy daughter__   __Derek Rupert Baker son__ .

2. GIFTS. I give these gifts in this Will, but to get a gift in this section the recipient must survive me except as otherwise stated below.

    I give __leather jacket I bought at the Georgia State Fair__ to __Anne J. Smith__ .

    I give __$5,000 and Ford Truck__ to __Loretta Marsha Baxter__ .

    I give __buildings, land, and fixtures at 63 Wentworth Road, Macon, Georgia,__
            to __Kenneth Alan Ford__ .

    I give __all real property and fixtures I own in Cherokee County in Georgia__ to
            __Amy Marie Fox and Pamela Sue Fox__ .

    I give __903 Iceberg Road, Anchorage, Alaska__ to __James Eric Hanson__ .

    I give __Irish jewelry and my wedding ring__ to __Mary Natalie Swanson__ .

    I give __all jewelry not given above__ to __Kay Baxter and Mary Baxter__ .

    I give __$781.35__ to __Mary Natalie Swanson and Kevin Kilby__ .

    I give __Wells Fargo acct ending in #8923__ to __Lawrence Deer a hunting buddy__ .

    I give __all spare tires and auto parts__ to __Victor Perez my mechanic__ .

3. SEPARATE WRITINGS. I may do writings separate from this Will to gift tangible personal property as allowed by state law, and all such writings should be followed. But any such writing not found within 90 days of my death is canceled and has no effect. A gift in such a writing to a person who does not survive me is canceled and has no effect. This Will does not revoke any such writings that now exist.

4. RESIDUE. The rest, residue, and remainder of my estate, and anything else, I give:
  a) to _____Ruth May Baker_____ who survive me and with persons just named who survive me taking the share of non-survivors, then if anything remains
  b) to 50% to Oscar Elliot Baker, 35% to Karen Lisa Lundy, 5% to Mary Sue Baker, and 10% to Luis Sanchez my friend_____ and if any of those just now named do not survive me their part goes to their lineal descendants per stirpes.

5. ADMINISTRATION. I name, nominate, and appoint ___Ruth May Baker_____ as Personal Representative including for me, my Will, and my estate.

6. GUARDIAN. I name ___Amanda Sue Brubaker_____ to be Guardian of any minor child of mine and also to have care, authority, custody, and other control of them (including as Guardian Of The Person). I also name this same person to be Conservator for any minor child and also to have care, control, and power over their property, money, and estate.

7. MISCELLANEOUS. The following applies to this Will and generally.
  In this Will no part left unfilled is a mistake including spaces in the residue clause.
  The facts support and I want Georgia state law to apply to this Will and my estate.
  I order that my just debts, funeral and related expenses, and taxes be paid as soon after my death as practical but only those items my Personal Representative chooses to pay.
  Any gift of money in this Will has priority over gifts in any separate writing.
  Priority of Will gifts of the same type is based on the order they are made in this Will.
  The words give and gift also means a devise, bequest, grant, legacy, or similar.
  I am intentionally not providing by Will or other ways for some family, including I am not providing for some children of mine and also children of a deceased child of mine.
  If a Will gift reasonably mentions survival then survival is an absolute condition and anti-lapse laws or similar provisions have no effect and without survival the gift lapses. Unless a Will gift specifies otherwise if a Will gift goes to multiple recipients if any do not survive me the part to them lapses and instead goes to other surviving recipients.
  No earlier transfer reduces a Will gift unless I usually called it a loan or advancement.
  In this Will any gendered word includes all genders, and the singular includes the plural and vice versa, and the word "they" can mean a single person or many persons.
  Unless a Will specifically says otherwise a secured debt including a mortgage or lien shall not be paid off including by a Personal Representative or in probate, and a recipient of a Will gift of property takes it subject to debts. Also, no recipient of property who may lose it or who pays to keep it may have my estate or other people pay or do exoneration.
  If I lost or no longer have an item in a Will specific gift then the gift is extinguished.
  I request and authorize any informal, summary, and quick probate or similar action. Any Personal Representative may act independently with no supervision of any court, including independent administration, and with no inventory, appraisal, or other action.
  I give any Personal Representative power to lease, sell, mortgage, convey, or keep

property including real property in a manner and time they deem helpful or proper. I give any Personal Representative authority to settle or pay claims or debts in the time and manner they choose. I give any Personal Representative all powers and authority that may be given by statute or common law in any jurisdiction, including powers and authorities conferred by the Georgia Revised Probate Code of 1998 and Revised Georgia Trust Code of 2010, as amended, plus Georgia Code §§ 53-12-261 and 263 et seq., as amended.

Any Guardian of any type, Conservator, Custodian, or other person managing a minor's property or money may use or invade the principal and sell property without court action.

The residue includes lapsed or failed gifts, insurance paid to the estate, digital assets, inheritances owed me, and all I had power of appointment or testamentary disposition over.

Any Personal Representative may access, manage, delete, modify, transfer, and otherwise control any digital accounts and assets I had any interest in or power over.

Any Personal Representative, Executor, Administrator, Guardian of any type like for a person or estate, Conservator, Custodian, and any other fiduciary under this Will or otherwise shall qualify and serve without bond, surety, security, surety bond, or similar.

If evidence does not show it likely a person survived me by 120 hours (5 days) then for this Will and my estate they shall be deemed in all ways as having died before me.

Any Personal Representative may at any time transfer money or property of a minor under age 18 to a Custodian to act under the Georgia Uniform Transfers to Minors Act or similar law anywhere, and may pick a person to be Custodian including themselves.

If part of this Will is invalid or unenforceable other provisions shall remain in effect.

TESTATOR

IN WITNESS WHEREOF and in the presence of two witnesses, who are acting as witnesses at my request, in my presence and in the presence of each other, I hereunto sign my name on the _15th_ day of _March_, 20_19_.

Paul Brian Baker
Signature of Testator

WITNESSES

The foregoing instrument was signed by the Testator in our presence and declared by the Testator to be the Testator's Will, and we, the undersigned witnesses, sign our names hereunto as witnesses at the request and in the presence of the Testator, and in the presence of each other on the _15th_ day of _March_, 20_19_.

Olivia Anna Paulson   82 Forest Road, Atlanta, GA 30305
Signature of Witness   Address of Witness

Matthew John Paulson   82 Forest Road, Atlanta, GA 30305
Signature of Witness   Address of Witness

Sample Filled Out Form : Will (Guardian)
with Gifts section left unused and, then, the Residue Clause done only using 2nd space so as to gift to all branches of person's descendants equally

LAST WILL AND TESTAMENT

I, __Thomas Roger Tedford__ of __Cobb County__, Georgia, do revoke all prior Wills and testamentary documents and do make, publish, and declare this as my Will. I am of sound mind and under no duress or undue influence and act voluntarily.

1. LIVING SPOUSE AND CHILDREN. To show I am mentally fit and have sufficient memory to do a Will I do say I now have the following living spouse and living children:

__Mary Paula Tedford my daughter__   __Gina Lola Smith my daughter__

_____.

2. GIFTS. I give these gifts in this Will, but to get a gift in this section the recipient must survive me except as otherwise stated below.

I give _____ to _____.
I give _____ to _____.
I give _____ to _____.
I give _____ to _____.
I give _____ to _____.
I give _____ to _____.
I give _____ to _____.
I give _____ to _____.
I give _____ to _____.

3. SEPARATE WRITINGS. I may do writings separate from this Will to gift tangible personal property as allowed by state law, and all such writings should be followed. But any such writing not found within 90 days of my death is canceled and has no effect. A gift in such a writing to a person who does not survive me is canceled and has no effect. This Will does not revoke any such writings that now exist.

4. RESIDUE. The rest, residue, and remainder of my estate, and anything else, I give:

   a) to _____ who survive me and with persons just named who survive me taking the share of non-survivors, then if anything remains

   b) to <u>Brian Alan Tedford my deceased son,   Mary Paula Tedford my daughter,   and Gina Lola Smith my daughter</u>   and if any of those just now named do not survive me their part goes to their lineal descendants per stirpes.

5. ADMINISTRATION. I name, nominate, and appoint <u>Mary Paula Tedford</u> as Personal Representative including for me, my Will, and my estate.

6. MISCELLANEOUS. The following applies to this Will and generally.

   In this Will no part left unfilled is a mistake including spaces in the residue clause.

   The facts support and I want Georgia state law to apply to this Will and my estate.

   I order that my just debts, funeral and related expenses, and taxes be paid as soon after my death as practical but only those items my Personal Representative chooses to pay.

   Any gift of money in this Will has priority over gifts in any separate writing.

   Priority of Will gifts of the same type is based on the order they are made in this Will.

   The words give and gift also means a devise, bequest, grant, legacy, or similar.

   I am intentionally not providing by Will or other ways for some family, including I am not providing for some children of mine and also children of a deceased child of mine.

   If a Will gift reasonably mentions survival then survival is an absolute condition and anti-lapse laws or similar provisions have no effect and without survival the gift lapses. Unless a Will gift specifies otherwise if a Will gift goes to multiple recipients if any do not survive me the part to them lapses and instead goes to other surviving recipients.

   No earlier transfer reduces a Will gift unless I usually called it a loan or advancement.

   In this Will any gendered word includes all genders, and the singular includes the plural and vice versa, and the word "they" can mean a single person or many persons.

   Unless a Will specifically says otherwise a secured debt including a mortgage or lien shall not be paid off including by a Personal Representative or in probate, and a recipient of a Will gift of property takes it subject to debts. Also, no recipient of property who may lose it or who pays to keep it may have my estate or other people pay or do exoneration.

   If I lost or no longer have an item in a Will specific gift then the gift is extinguished.

   I request and authorize any informal, summary, and quick probate or similar action. Any Personal Representative may act independently with no supervision of any court, including independent administration, and with no inventory, appraisal, or other action.

   I give any Personal Representative power to lease, sell, mortgage, convey, or keep property including real property in a manner and time they deem helpful or proper.

I give any Personal Representative authority to settle or pay claims or debts in the time and manner they choose. I give any Personal Representative all powers and authority that may be given by statute or common law in any jurisdiction, including powers and authorities

conferred by the Georgia Revised Probate Code of 1998 and Revised Georgia Trust Code of 2010, as amended, plus Georgia Code §§ 53-12-261 and 263 et seq., as amended.

Any Guardian of any type, Conservator, Custodian, or other person managing a minor's property or money may use or invade the principal and sell property without court action.

If context permits the terms Personal Representative and Executor and Administrator are interchangeable, Conservator and Guardian of the Estate and Guardian of Property and Custodian are interchangeable, and residue and residuary are interchangeable. Any such person may stand in the place of and have all powers like the others named here.

The residue includes lapsed or failed gifts, insurance paid to the estate, digital assets, inheritances owed me, and all I had power of appointment or testamentary disposition over.

Any Personal Representative may access, manage, delete, modify, transfer, and otherwise control any digital accounts and assets I had any interest in or power over.

Any Personal Representative, Executor, Administrator, Guardian of any type like for a person or estate, Conservator, Custodian, and any other fiduciary under this Will or otherwise shall qualify and serve without bond, surety, security, surety bond, or similar.

If evidence does not show it likely a person survived me by 120 hours (5 days) then for this Will and my estate they shall be deemed in all ways as having died before me.

Any Personal Representative may at any time transfer money or property of a minor under age 18 to a Custodian to act under the Georgia Uniform Transfers to Minors Act or similar law anywhere, and may pick a person to be Custodian including themselves.

If part of this Will is invalid or unenforceable other provisions shall remain in effect.

TESTATOR

IN WITNESS WHEREOF and in the presence of two witnesses, who are acting as witnesses at my request, in my presence and in the presence of each other, I hereunto sign my name on the _22nd_ day of _July_, 20_23_.

Thomas Roger Tedford
Signature of Testator

WITNESSES

The foregoing instrument was signed by the Testator in our presence and declared by the Testator to be the Testator's Will, and we, the undersigned witnesses, sign our names hereunto as witnesses at the request and in the presence of the Testator, and in the presence of each other on the _22nd_ day of _July_, 20_23_.

Maria Bonita Buena   101 Fox Rd., Apt. #35 Clayton, GA 30318
Signature of Witness   Address of Witness

Richard Max West   28 Miller Avenue, Pineville, GA 38124
Signature of Witness   Address of Witness

Sample Filled Out Form : Will (Standard)
with Will modified to have a 1 Part Residue Clause

LAST WILL AND TESTAMENT

I, _John David Smith_, of _Fulton County_, Georgia, do revoke all prior Wills and testamentary documents and do make, publish, and declare this as my Will. I am of sound mind and under no duress or undue influence and act voluntarily.

1. LIVING SPOUSE AND CHILDREN. To show I am mentally fit and have sufficient memory to do a Will I do say I now have the following living spouse and living children: _my son Adam Michael Smith_ .

2. GIFTS. I give these gifts in this Will, but to get a gift in this section the recipient must survive me except as otherwise stated below.

I give _$200_ to _each of my nieces and nephews so about $2,800 in total_ .

I give _$400_ to _Garner Food Shelf in Atlanta, Georgia by city hall_ .

I give _$340_ to _my old church Trinity Catholic Church in Pueblo, Colorado_ .

I give _____ to _____ .

I give _____ to _____ .

I give _____ to _____ .

I give _____ to _____ .

3. SEPARATE WRITINGS. I may do writings separate from this Will to gift tangible personal property as allowed by state law, and all such writings should be followed. But any such writing not found within 90 days of my death is canceled and has no effect. A gift in such a writing to a person who does not survive me is canceled and has no effect. This Will does not revoke any such writings that now exist.

4. RESIDUE. The rest, residue, and remainder of my estate, and anything else, I give to: _Adam Michael Smith and Judy Paula Ford my children_ who survive me and if any of those just named do not survive me their part goes to their lineal descendants per stirpes.

5. ADMINISTRATION. I name, nominate, and appoint ___Judy Paula Ford my sister___ as Personal Representative including for me, my Will, and my estate.

6. MISCELLANEOUS. The following applies to this Will and generally.

In this Will no part left unfilled is a mistake including spaces in the residue clause.

The facts support and I want Georgia state law to apply to this Will and my estate.

I order that my just debts, funeral and related expenses, and taxes be paid as soon after my death as practical but only those items my Personal Representative chooses to pay.

Any gift of money in this Will has priority over gifts in any separate writing.

Priority of Will gifts of the same type is based on the order they are made in this Will.

The words give and gift also means a devise, bequest, grant, legacy, or similar.

I am intentionally not providing by Will or other ways for some family, including I am not providing for some children of mine and also children of a deceased child of mine.

If a Will gift reasonably mentions survival then survival is an absolute condition and anti-lapse laws or similar provisions have no effect and without survival the gift lapses. Unless a Will gift specifies otherwise if a Will gift goes to multiple recipients if any do not survive me the part to them lapses and instead goes to other surviving recipients.

No earlier transfer reduces a Will gift unless I usually called it a loan or advancement.

In this Will any gendered word includes all genders, and the singular includes the plural and vice versa, and the word "they" can mean a single person or many persons.

Unless a Will specifically says otherwise a secured debt including a mortgage or lien shall not be paid off including by a Personal Representative or in probate, and a recipient of a Will gift of property takes it subject to debts. Also, no recipient of property who may lose it or who pays to keep it may have my estate or other people pay or do exoneration.

If I lost or no longer have an item in a Will specific gift then the gift is extinguished.

I request and authorize any informal, summary, and quick probate or similar action. Any Personal Representative may act independently with no supervision of any court, including independent administration, and with no inventory, appraisal, or other action.

I give any Personal Representative power to lease, sell, mortgage, convey, or keep property including real property in a manner and time they deem helpful or proper. I give any Personal Representative authority to settle or pay claims or debts in the time and manner they choose. I give any Personal Representative all powers and authority that may be given by statute or common law in any jurisdiction, including powers and authorities conferred by the Georgia Revised Probate Code of 1998 and Revised Georgia Trust Code of 2010, as amended, plus Georgia Code §§ 53-12-261 and 263 et seq., as amended.

Any Guardian of any type, Conservator, Custodian, or other person managing a minor's property or money may use or invade the principal and sell property without court action.

If context permits the terms Personal Representative and Executor and Administrator are interchangeable, Conservator and Guardian of the Estate and Guardian of Property and Custodian are interchangeable, and residue and residuary are interchangeable. Any such person may stand in the place of and have all powers like the others named here.

The residue includes lapsed or failed gifts, insurance paid to the estate, digital assets, inheritances owed me, and all I had power of appointment or testamentary disposition over.

Any Personal Representative may access, manage, delete, modify, transfer, and otherwise control any digital accounts and assets I had any interest in or power over.

Any Personal Representative, Executor, Administrator, Guardian of any type like for a person or estate, Conservator, Custodian, and any other fiduciary under this Will or otherwise shall qualify and serve without bond, surety, security, surety bond, or similar.

If evidence does not show it likely a person survived me by 120 hours (5 days) then for this Will and my estate they shall be deemed in all ways as having died before me.

Any Personal Representative may at any time transfer money or property of a minor under age 18 to a Custodian to act under the Georgia Uniform Transfers to Minors Act or similar law anywhere, and may pick a person to be Custodian including themselves.

If part of this Will is invalid or unenforceable other provisions shall remain in effect.

TESTATOR

IN WITNESS WHEREOF and in the presence of two witnesses, who are acting as witnesses at my request, in my presence and in the presence of each other, I hereunto sign my name on the _30th_ day of _December_, 20_19_.

John David Smith
Signature of Testator

WITNESSES

The foregoing instrument was signed by the Testator in our presence and declared by the Testator to be the Testator's Will, and we, the undersigned witnesses, sign our names hereunto as witnesses at the request and in the presence of the Testator, and in the presence of each other on the _30th_ day of _December_, 20_19_.

Mark Elliot Potter   24 Pine St., Sherwood, GA 30304
Signature of Witness   Address of Witness

Ann Paula Blom   80 Oak Ave., Edison, Georgia 31371
Signature of Witness   Address of Witness

Sample Filled Out Form : Self-Proving Affidavit

SELF-PROVING AFFIDAVIT

STATE OF GEORGIA

COUNTY OF __FULTON COUNTY__

   Before me, the undersigned authority, on this day personally appeared __John David Smith__ (testator), __Mark Elliot Potter__ (witness), and __Ann Paula Blom__ (witness), known to me to be the testator and the witnesses, respectively, whose names are subscribed to the annexed or foregoing instrument in their respective capacities, and all of said individuals being by me duly sworn, __John David Smith__, testator, declared to me and to the witnesses in my presence that said instrument is the last will and testament and that the testator had willingly made and executed it as a free act and deed for the purposes expressed therein. The witnesses, each on oath, stated to me in the presence and hearing of the testator that the testator had declared to them that the instrument is the testator's last will and testament and that the testator executed the instrument as such and wished each of them to sign it as a witness; and under oath each witness stated further that the witness had signed the same as witness in the presence of the testator and at the testator's request; that the testator was 14 years of age or over and of sound mind; and that each of the witnesses was then at least 14 years of age.

John David Smith
Testator

Mark Elliot Potter
Witness

Ann Paula Blom
Witness

Sworn to and subscribed before me by __John David Smith__, testator, and sworn to and subscribed before me by __Mark Elliot Potter__ and __Ann Paula Blom__ witnesses, this __30th__ day of __December__, 20__19__.

[NOTARY SEAL OR STAMP]

Jonathan Montgomery
Notary Public

TANGIBLE PERSONAL PROPERTY GIFT LIST

In this writing are gifts of tangible personal property to occur at my death including as provided by Georgia Code § 53-4-5. But this writing if not found by someone in the 90 days after my death is canceled and shall have no effect at all.

I may do many pages of these writings which should all be seen as one document. If there are conflicts among such writings the provisions of the more recent writing shall cancel the inconsistent provisions of a prior writing.

If a person getting a gift below does not survive me such gift is void and canceled.

DESCRIPTION OF PROPERTY	NAME OF PERSONS TO GET PROPERTY
1998 Ford Truck	to Kevin Swenson
1.3 carat diamond ring + Irish rings	to Ann Sue Reed
14 ft power boat + kayak + paddles	to Luke Wheeler
Amish style bench	to Reba Stewart
glass table, telescope, umbrellas	to Wendy Stewart
Irish wood cups, oak platter, red vase	to Mary and Cindy Lott
painting of sailboat in storm	to Mary Lott
chainsaw with number 382937	to Mary Lott
chainsaw with number 89930	to Matt Smith
antique lanterns + repair kits	to Sue Park maid at Hart Hotel
lamp kept on porch	to Mary Kay Poppler
sewing machines	to Mary Kay Poppler
rocking chair bought in Oregon	to Don Winkler boat mechanic
all fishing poles and fishing nets	to Joe "Fish" Hoss, fishing pal
hats at cabin	to Ken Baker
all clothing except hats at cabin	to Melissa and Arthur Smith
	to
	to
	to

DATE: 8-15-2024   SIGNED: *John David Smith*

www.ingramcontent.com/pod-product-compliance
Lightning Source LLC
Chambersburg PA
CBHW060415220526
45465CB00008B/2891